AUTHENTIC FOOD QUEST
Argentina

A Guide to Eat Your Way Authentically Through Argentina

ROSEMARY KIMANI & CLAIRE ROUGER

Authentic Food Quest Argentina
A Guide To Eat Your Way Authentically Through Argentina

Copyright © 2016 Rosemary Kimani and Claire Rouger

All Rights Reserved.
No part of this publication may be reproduced or transmitted in any form or by any means, mechanical or electronic, including photocopying and recording, or by any information storage or retrieval system, without prior written permission of the copyright owners, except for the use of brief quotations in reviews.

For permission requests, write to the publisher at contact@authenticfoodquest.com or via authenticfoodquest.com

ISBN: 978-0-9978101-1-0 (paperback)
978-0-9978101-0-3 (ebook)

Editor: Emily Kidd, EmilyKidd.com
Text design and layout: Elena Reznikova
Cover design: http://bookcover.biz

Cover Images Photo Credits:
Alfajores - Authentic Food Quest
Empanadas - Authentic Food Quest
Grilling - The Vines of Mendoza

Photography by Authentic Food Quest, except where otherwise noted.

Get Your Free Ebook
To get tips on how to find authentic food on your travels, get your free ebook:
The Five Best Ways To Find Authentic Food While Traveling
at authenticfoodquest.com

Table of Contents

Introduction *with Francis Mallmann* 4
Our Quest for Authentic Food in Argentina 7
How To Use This Book 9

1. TERROIR: Learning the "Lay of the Land" for Authentic Food in Argentina 10
- Welcome to Argentina 10
- Tips for Foodie Travelers in Argentina 11
- How to Eat and Shop Like a Local 16
- Unique Culinary Experiences in Argentina 21

2. SAVOR THIS: Top Authentic Food & Drinks Not to Be Missed on Your Travels 25
- Authentic Specialities 25
- Street Food 53
- Desserts (Postres) 58
- Unique Produce 67
- Beverages 70

3. DESTINATIONS: Where To Eat Across Argentina 77
- Buenos Aires & the Pampas 77
- The Wine Regions 92
- The Andean Northwest Region 110
- Patagonia & the Lake Region 116

4. RESOURCES: What You Should Know About Traveling in Argentina 129
- Culinary Culture in Argentina and Beyond 129
- Practical Travel Resources 130
- Health and Fitness While Traveling 134

Acknowledgements 137
About the Authors 138

Introduction

with Francis Mallmann

"Food is an adventure. A discovery of new flavors. An introduction to new ingredients. An embracing of new cultures. Food and travel inspire connections."

—Excerpt from our charter
(AuthenticFoodQuest.com/charter)

Tucked in the bright La Boca neighborhood of Buenos Aires is a red building with arched windows that you might simply walk by if you were unaware of the treasure inside. Elegant, colorful, and signless, Patagonia Sur is an icon in Argentine food culture, and we were blessed to be sitting at its single dining table with Francis Mallmann.

The most renowned chef in Argentina, Mallmann was featured in the Netflix documentary *Chef's Table*. He spoke to us about how Argentine chefs are shaping the food culture today.

"The future for authenticity and a return to traditional roots is on the horizon, and we are making a comeback," he said. "Every country has to explore and go back to its roots and mirror those images back to its people through its cooking."

His idea highlights the deep connections between food, place, people, and passion. As longtime travelers, this quote spoke to us: we can think of no better way to connect with a new place than through food.

We wrote this book so you can do the same.

We are Rosemary Kimani and Claire Rouger, partners and co-founders of **AuthenticFoodQuest.com**. We created Authentic Food Quest to inspire you to travel through authentic food.

As travelers, we have lived in Chicago, Paris and Los Angeles and have visited more than 27 countries. We have often seen that while most travelers are craving to experience the local specialities on their travels, they don't have access to reliable and trustworthy information, and as a result, end up disappointed.

Claire and Rosemary with Francis Mallmann at Patagonia Sur Restaurant, Buenos Aires, August 28th, 2015.

Authentic food experiences are the perfect way to explore Argentina, and we created this guide to help you discover them.

Francis Mallmann told us that particularly in Argentina, food can unlock deeper connections with people. "The biggest quality of Argentina for me is that feeling of sharing a meal," he told us at his dinner table. "And that is the true reason to eat and drink something delicious. [It] is to share. For me, it is the only reason."

> *"Lunch is important. Dinner is important and you sit down for lunch and you sit down for dinner. And you talk! And after lunch or dinner you spend an hour talking about something."*
>
> —Francis Mallmann

Imagine the people you might connect with if you ate like an Argentine!

Food can also take you on a journey through the landscape. "One of the biggest beauties of our fruits and vegetables are the ones that grow in the Andes at 4,000 meters (13,000 feet)," Mallmann said.

"The potatoes, pumpkins, peaches, plums that grow at that altitude—you look at them, they don't look nice, but they are delicious . . . they struggle to survive and concentrate a lot of taste because of that.

"It is quite romantic because if you think about a plant without water in harsh conditions, it feels like it is going to die. So, what does it do? It sends everything to the fruit where the grains grow because that is where the future comes from.

"Then we have good lamb and fish in the south. In the Andes and in the north of Argentina we have incredible goat. Try peppers dried in the sun. *Humitas* and *empanadas*. Every province has its own regional different variety."

We discovered all these specialties on our travels, and have left our notes for you. Perhaps the greatest joy of traveling this way is the simplicity of such full experiences in a single bite.

"As we grow older, the most beautiful path is simplicity and the most difficult one," Mallmann said. "I have to admit that it is very difficult to make it good if it is simple."

And yet, Francis Mallmann is devoted to simplicity. "The simpler the food, the more perfect the ingredients have to be. When you have bad ingredients you make sauces, you complicate things. You hide things. When I make a steak with salt and a boiled potato, it has to be very perfect for you to enjoy it. The meat, the salt, that potato, a little olive oil, parsley; that's all we need, really! People think that is so easy. It is not so easy, because temperatures are important. Everything has to be really perfect. So simple, so perfect."

This is what we offer you in our guide: a journey through food that is so simple, so perfect, that you will get to know this place Argentines call home.

Savor the Adventure!

Our Quest for Authentic Food in Argentina

A Journey Through Food In Argentina

Our journey through food in Argentina began as a quest to understand the local and authentic dishes of the region. What began as a passion, a way of life and a dream culminated in us leaving our corporate careers in mid 2015 and embarking on a travel adventure to discover authentic food around the world.

We chose to start our quest in Argentina. We spent six months in South America diving into "slow travel" and seeking out the local and authentic dishes of the different countries.

But our adventure wasn't finished there. This is the first book of a series aimed at inspiring you to travel through authentic food.

Your trip to Argentina will more than likely involve a stop in Buenos Aires, the capital. While you will find the major regional specialities available, we encourage you to leave the city and explore the specialities from the regions they come from.

Only by leaving the capital will you see as we did, the pride and command chefs of all calibers have with the native ingredients. (In the **Resources**, you will find tributes to select chefs we were inspired by across the country.)

Our food itinerary was created and shaped by the many conversations we had with locals and experts. They consistently recommended the following regions:

- **Buenos Aires** and **The Pampas**
- **The Wine Regions:** Mendoza and Cafayate
- **The Andean Northwest:** Salta and Jujuy
- **Patagonia and the Lake Region:** Bariloche, El Calafate, and Ushuaia

We traversed the country visiting the different regions, primarily using the long haul bus system. In total, we covered over 10,500 kilometers (over 6,560 miles). In each of the regions we visited, we spent ten to thirty days.

We used this time to become familiar with the area, connect with the locals, visit the farmers markets and food stores as well as visit some cultural and historical sites. Our goal was to travel slowly and forge deep connections with the place and people. Staying with locals through Airbnb gave us a deeper experience and immediate entry into the local rhythm and pace.

Our Approach to Authentic Eating in Argentina

The way we approached understanding and discovering the local and authentic dishes in Argentina was by following these four simple steps:

1. We started out by researching the local foods ahead of time. We spent time doing extensive online research, reading articles, blog posts and books about the food in Argentina. (Luckily for you, we've distilled that research in this guide.)

2. We connected with locals prior to leaving for Argentina and also while in the country. The locals we met were open and proudly shared their favorite authentic dishes with us. They shared stories, memories and the places to experience the dishes.

3. We visited numerous farmers markets and local food stores to see the produce in season as well as the unique and regional specialities.

4. We interviewed local experts who helped us understand the local specialities and their cultural significance. These experts included vendors at the farmers markets, restaurant owners and chefs as well as locals that we met along our journey.

We offer that wisdom to you. In the following pages, you will find the emblematic dishes and traditional drinks outlined. You will also find an overview of the best farmers markets and local food stores to visit, along with addresses of the local restaurants where you can try the authentic dishes on your travels.

Interspersed throughout the book are stories, tips and fun facts about the regional dishes. You will also find a list of unique foodie activities such as cooking classes, tours, and food festivals to enhance your overall experience.

We also include a couple of iconic recipes, and tips for travelers who are vegetarian or gluten-free: everything you need to make your culinary adventure through Argentina much more enjoyable.

Think of this book as a complement to your travel guide. Most guides present a cursory overview on the local dishes; here you get an exclusive focus on the authentic and regional specialities.

BUEN PROVENCHO!

How To Use This Book

This book is broken into four main parts:

1. TERROIR

TERROIR provides a "lay of the land" of what to expect on your culinary trip in Argentina.

- You will find a summary of Argentine cuisine and helpful food-related tips.
- We include Spanish vocabulary and phrases to use when ordering your meals.
- Learn where to shop like locals, and discover the different types of stores and restaurants you can expect to find.
- This part ends with food-related activities you will find in Argentina such as cooking classes, food tours, and more. It includes a calendar of food and drink festivals you should attend.

2. SAVOR THIS

SAVOR THIS dives into the authentic specialities you must not miss.

- Find 50+ local and traditional specialities broken down into dishes, desserts, street food, unique produce and local beverages. As the dishes are mentioned throughout this book, they will appear in bold; when you see highlighted food terms, feel free to return to the Savor This section to read more about them.
- In this section you will also find unique tips from experts we interviewed, and videos with locals discussing some of the traditional specialities.

3. DESTINATIONS

DESTINATIONS are categorized into the four major geographic regions we visited.

- For each region, we include the best markets and local stores to shop.
- Try local specialities at the best restaurants: we include addresses, contact information, and hours of operation at our favorite eateries. Note that many websites for Argentine restaurants are in Spanish, but on most devices, Google Translate will automatically ask if you would like it converted to English.
- Find unique food experiences, like live cooking demonstrations in the open-air markets, festivals and wine tastings.

4. RESOURCES

RESOURCES contains additional necessary odds and ends for making your trip a success.

- We showcase local chefs who are building the Argentine food scene.
- Nervous about travel, visas, and changing money? We have quick practical tips.
- As devoted foodies, we are also devoted to our health, and include travel fitness pointers from our blog at AuthenticFoodQuest.com.

Ultimately, this book provides a written and visual record of the authentic food experiences in Argentina. The experience comes to life when you taste these specialities and open yourself up to new foods, flavors and textures.

For more links and resources visit: **authenticfoodquest.com/argentinabook**

1. TERROIR

Learning the "Lay of the Land" for Authentic Food in Argentina

Welcome to Argentina

Argentina, the eighth largest country in the world, is a spectacular country and a popular destination in South America. Revel at the natural beauty of Iguazu waterfalls, sip on the famous Malbec wine in Mendoza or journey through Patagonia to Ushuaia, the southernmost city in the world. Then there is tango dancing, the nomadic horse culture of the *gauchos* and, of course, the world-famous beef. Whether you love adventure, nature, culture or food, you will find your place in Argentina.

Argentina General Map, Based on OCHA Map

The capital, Buenos Aires, is also the largest city in Argentina, home to about a third of the 40 million residents. The culture is incredibly diverse, as you will see reflected in its cuisine. It is considered one of the most elegant cities in South America and jokingly referred to as the "Paris of South America."

Argentine Cuisine

It is not easy to identify or define "Argentine cuisine." Visitors will be surprised at the eclectic mix of indigenous flavors with a European palate from Italian, German, and Spanish immigrants. The food landscape goes well beyond the famous beef and many European inspired dishes have a distinctive Argentine twist.

Food in Argentina is revered, celebrated and looked up to. There is a culture around eating and sharing meals. Food brings people together to enjoy the food, the flavors and the social connections. These are cherished moments.

Great feasts like the **asado** of *gaucho* culture, and the **curanto** of Patagonia become opportunities for communities to bind together. Be sure to wash everything down with local and traditional beverages like the world famous **Malbec** wine and **mate** tea. Always finish with a *postres*; Argentines have a cultural love affair with sweets as much as good food.

Different regions of Argentina use local produce that are specific to the area, and throughout this book you will see we have noted where certain dishes come from. The Savor This section of this book goes into more detail on the different local and regional specialities.

Tips for Foodie Travelers in Argentina

Eating hours

Lunch is typically eaten between 1pm to 3pm, and then most restaurants close for *siesta*. Many restaurants are open again by 7pm or 8pm for dinner, but you will usually find tourists at these hours. To eat with the locals, plan on going to dinner after 9pm; peak hours are between 10pm and 11:30pm. Restaurants still have customers at their tables at 2:00 in the morning.

Media tarde or *merienda*, which roughly translates to "afternoon tea," is a great way to manage your hunger before dinner. The afternoon tea typically consists of tea, coffee, **mate** or **beer** with *medialunas*, *tostadas* or other snacks.

Picada in Argentina is basically finger food, or hors d'oeuvres. It is an Argentine tradition to serve "artfully arranged" cold cuts, cheese, olives and more to enjoy with wine and beer. A *picada* can be an appetizer before an **asado**, a late night snack with friends, something to nibble on at a bar or pub, or a meal of its own.

Tipping in Argentina

In Argentina, the tip is called *propina* and it is not mandatory at restaurants, though it is desirable. It is customary to tip about 10% of the bill. If the service is not great, you can leave less or nothing at all. On the other hand, if the service was fabulous, you want to leave more than 10%. Your generosity will be appreciated.

Some restaurants charge a *cubierto*, which is a cover charge anywhere from 10 to 20 pesos. This cover charge is not a tip and includes paying for the cutlery, bread, placemats, etc. It's a clever way of charging for nothing; the money goes directly to the restaurant and is not part of the tip, nor does it go to the waitstaff. You will still need to leave a tip. If you don't like the *cubierto* charge, be sure to pay careful attention to the fine print on the menu.

When paying for meals, be prepared with cash in hand. In the larger cities and towns, you will find restaurants that accept major credit cards. Restaurants do not have a "tip" section on credit card receipts, so if you are planning on paying for the meal with plastic, be sure to bring cash to pay the tip separately.

When paying for the bill or tipping in cash, be sure not to leave the money on the table and walk away; it is quite possible that it can be snagged by someone other than your server, so give the *propina* directly to them.

Ordering water

Automatically getting served water at your table is not typical. You will have to ask for it. When you order water, you will get a bottle. If you want flat water, be sure to ask for *sin gas*. If you prefer sparking mineral water, ask for *con gas*. The most popular brand of mineral water is called **Villavicencio**.

Soda bottle

Instead of mineral water, try what Argentines call "soda." It is cold water injected with carbon dioxide. The carbon dioxide gives it a fresh, fizzy taste. The water is served in either vintage Seltzer bottles or plastic bottles. You will find mostly plastic siphon bottles. Place a glass to the nozzle, push the lever down, and enjoy your fresh, fizzy water.

Order the "menu of the day"

Get the best eating experience on your travels by ordering the *menú del dia* or *menú ejecutivo*. These are value priced meals that are typically served at lunch and consist of a starter, main course, and dessert for a fixed price. Look for this option to not only enjoy a fresh and local meal, but to also save on your budget.

The dining experience

The dining experience is a drawn-out activity in Argentina. The concept of 'quick-turnover' of tables does not exist. You will notice that the waitstaff don't hover around you much. They just don't want to make you feel hurried. If you need to get the waiter's attention it is perfectly acceptable to say, in a casual tone, "*señor*" or "*señora*", "*la cuenta, por favor*" for the bill.

Leftovers

Asking to take home leftovers from a restaurant is not very common in Argentina. In the capital of Buenos Aires, it might raise eyebrows, but restaurants—particularly those that cater to tourists—will pack your food to go. Outside of the capital, you may get surprised looks for asking for a take-away box. If you want to take home your leftovers regardless of the custom, say that it is for your pet—that is considered less embarrassing.

Eating in public

Eating on public transportation or on the street is generally frowned upon. The same goes for drinking alcohol in public places. You will notice some exceptions with **mate** or with small bites like *empanadas* if one is rushed or in a hurry.

Vegetarians

Vegetarians, don't despair. Even in Argentina, famous for it's beef, you will still be able to eat vegetarian versions of many of the local and authentic specialities. You will find vegetarian *empanadas* for a quick snack, **pizza** topped with vegetables, **pasta**, salads, **quinoa** sandwiches, *milanesa* made with soy and more.

Although we are not vegetarian, we enjoyed fresh and delicious meals at several vegetarian restaurants in Buenos Aires, Mendoza and Salta. As a vegetarian, you will be able to find meals to satisfy your tastes. Throughout the Savor This section, we will mark dishes that can be made vegetarian.

For a more detailed guide to vegetarian restaurants in Buenos Aires, check out the Guia Oleo guide to "Vegetarian Food in Buenos Aires: 50 unmissable options."

http://dixit.guiaoleo.com.ar/
cocina-vegetariana-50-opciones-imperdibles-2/

Another great resource for vegetarian restaurants across Argentina is the website HappyCow, which allows you to browse by city:

http://www.happycow.net/south_america/argentina

Gluten-Free Options

If you suffer from Celiac disease or are gluten-sensitive, you can still enjoy Argentina's amazing food. Look for the symbol above at grocery stores: Sin

T.A.C.C (*sin trigo, avena, cebada and centeno*) translates to "free of wheat, oats, barley and rye."

You will find gluten-free products at most grocery stores in Buenos Aires and the larger cities as well at *dietéticas* (health stores). Authentic food is still within your reach with the availability of gluten-free **empanadas**, **pizza** and even **alfajores** cookies.

With the growing awareness of Celiac disease you will find restaurants offering some gluten-free menu options. Don't hesitate to ask restaurants to prepare meals to accommodate your dietary restrictions.

Though this site is in Spanish, you can find a listing of restaurants with gluten-free options across Argentina here: **http://www.celiaco.org.ar/index.php/restaurantes**

Food Safety in Argentina

Argentina is a modern country with good hygiene and sanitary conditions. Restaurants provide relatively good hygiene and tap water is for the most part safe to drink across the country.

Food from street vendors and farmers markets is safe to eat. Nonetheless, always use caution when buying prepared meals from any vendors. In many places you will find one person that handles the money while another person handles the food. This is a good thing as it helps prevent the spread of germs.

10 HEALTHY HABITS ON YOUR TRAVELS IN ARGENTINA

1. Give yourself time to adjust before trying new and exotic foods.
2. Observe where and when the locals eat and adopt the local eating rhythm.
3. Choose the popular food vendors with long lines and families. When you see children and the elderly eating at food stalls, this is a good sign that those stalls have quality and healthy food.
4. Make sure the person who is handling the food is not the same person handling the money.
5. Choose food that is cooked and is served hot.
6. Wash your hands before eating or handling food.
7. Wash fruits and vegetables prior to eating them.
8. When in doubt, don't drink tap water. Instead buy bottled water or make sure the water is boiled or filtered.
9. When in doubt do not ask for ice cubes for your beverages.
10. Use your own cutlery to ensure hygiene. We always carry a spork (spoon fork combo) and would use it if in doubt.

Culinary Terms & Vocabulary

You will find English spoken in many places in Buenos Aires, but as you leave the Capital you will want to familiarize yourself with these key food related terms.

CULINARY TERMS & VOCABULARY	
Parrilla	Barbecue / Steakhouse
A la plancha	Grilled
Asado	Barbecue
Ahumado	Smoked
Al Horno	Baked/ Roasted
Picante	Hot/Spicy
Cerdo	Pork
Carne de Vaca	Beef
Pollo	Chicken
Pescado	Fish
Cordero	Lamb
Verdura	Vegetables
Huevo	Egg
Zanahoria	Carrot
Lechuga	Lettuce
Cebolla	Onion
Zapallitos	Zucchini
Fruta	Fruit
Papas	Potatoes
Frutilla	Strawberry
Manzana	Apple
Naranja	Orange
Queso	Cheese
Manteca	Butter
Aceite	Oil
Azucar	Sugar
Pan	Bread
Pimienta	Pepper
Sal	Salt
Desayuno	Breakfast
Almuerzo	Lunch
Cena	Dinner
Copa	Glass for wine
Botella	Bottle
Agua	Water
Soda	Sparkling water
Caliente	Warm/hot
Frio	Cold

CULINARY TERMS & VOCABULARY	
Vaso	Glass for water
Bebidas	Beverages
Cerveza	Beer
Platos Principales	Main Meal / Entrées
Entrada	Starter
Postres	Desserts
The check, please, *La cuenta, por favor*	
White wine, *vino blanco* / Red wine, *vino tinto*	
What is the local food speciality? *¿Cuál es la comida típica local?*	
What is the speciality of the restaurant? *¿Cuál es la especialidad de la casa?*	
I am vegetarian, *Soy vegetariano/a* Do you have vegetarian food? *¿Tienen comida vegetariana?*	
That was delicious, *Estaba riquisimo*	

In the **Savor This** section, you will find detailed information on the meat cuts and the terms used to describe them, as well as differences between specific dishes listed here.

How to Eat and Shop Like a Local

To appreciate and understand what is local in Argentina, you want to shop like the locals and eat where the locals eat. The Destinations section of this book goes into the specific addresses and locations broken out by region, but here we'll give you an overview of the different types of markets, food stores, restaurants and food related activities you can expect to find in Argentina.

USE THE ICONS BELOW TO QUICKLY IDENTIFY THE PLACES AND ACTIVITIES

Farmers Market | Food Stores | Restaurants | Street Food Vendors | Unique Culinary Experiences

 ## Farmers Markets

One of the best ways to find authentic and local food in Argentina is to visit the markets. The markets are somewhat different than typical markets you would find in Europe or North America.

There are three types of farmers markets: the organic farmers markets, the permanent indoor markets, and the temporary or "mobile" markets. This is mostly true for Buenos Aires; outside of the capital, you will mostly find permanent farmers markets.

Organic Farmers Markets

Farmers Market: Mercado de San Telmo, Buenos Aires

Organic farmers markets are a growing trend in Argentina driven by a search for healthier foods and organic products. You will find several niche markets that sell only organic foods in Buenos Aires. These markets tend to be small with vendors selling fruits, vegetables, and locally made organic products. Given the size and limited options, do not expect to fill your entire shopping cart with all your vegetables and fruits for the week.

Permanent Farmers Markets

This group of farmers markets are permanent and covered (as opposed to open-air markets). You will find many permanent and covered markets across the country. These are often referred to as *Mercado Central* or *Mercado Municipal*. Your best bet to find the market closest to you is to ask locals in your neighborhood.

Temporary or "Mobile" Farmers Markets

These are "mobile" farmers markets that move around to different locations around the city. The most popular and trendy market is the Buenos Aires Market, for which there is a write up in Destinations. When looking for the local markets, don't forget to ask residents about these temporary markets.

 ## Food Stores

The Big Stores

There are many options for supermarkets across Argentina. The two most popular national chains are Carrefour and Jumbo. You will also find regional chains such as La Anonima, Supermercado, Disco and Todo. We list major supermarkets in the different regions in **Destinations**.

The Local Specialty Stores

The local food stores in Argentina are quite an experience and one that you should explore on your trip. They are much smaller than the supermarkets, giving you the opportunity to interact with the owners and connect with locals.

Following are the different types of stores you can expect in the country.

Panaderías

Panaderías are bakeries, and you will find them at pretty much at every corner. The focus is bread and sweet pastries, although some *panaderías* also sell pre-packaged meals to go that can satisfy a lunch or dinner at home.

Surprisingly, bread is often sold as little buns called *boletos*. These are quite delicious and they are often made fresh daily. They are typically sold by the kilo. If you are an avid lover of sweet pastries, you will find all types of *facturas* on display. Grab a basket and choose a couple, including the ones filled with *dulce de leche*. Don't miss visiting a *panadería* on your trip to Argentina.

Local Food Store, Buenos Aires

Verdulerías y Fruterías

Verdulerías y Fruterías are corner groceries stores that sell fresh fruits and vegetables. You will find them literally at every corner across the country. Some are large stores, while the vast majority are smaller mom and pop shops.

Here you will find great selections of high quality vegetables and fruits at very affordable prices. One great benefit of *verdulerías y fruterías* is that they typically sell seasonal vegetables and fruits. By buying what is in season, you will enjoy the most delicious produce with the fullest flavors.

Carnicerías

Carnicerías can be best described as local butchers. At these stores, you will find different cuts of beef similar to the ones you can enjoy at a *parrilla* (local steakhouse). Sometimes you will find *verdulerías* combined with *carnicerías*. Other times, you will find *carnicerías* as stand alone stores. The beef is generally the main meat on display, though you will also find sausages, poultry, and cured meats.

The Dietética

Dietéticas are like health food stores. You will find them mostly in the larger cities, with Buenos Aires having the largest concentration of stores. If you are looking for speciality products, including vegetarian and gluten-free items, this is a great option.

You will also find great raw sugar, artisanal honey, spices and all sorts of different grains and dried fruits. When it comes to milk, you will find only cow's milk at the supermarkets. You will need to go to the *dietética* for soy milk, and very rarely will you find almond milk.

Pasta Stores

One of the most popular types of speciality stores in Argentina are the pasta stores. As Argentina's cuisine has been heavily influenced by Italians, you will find many options of places to buy fresh pasta. No need to buy dry pasta from the supermarkets. Instead, visit any of the stores highlighted in Destinations and prepare a simple and delicious meal.

Cheese and Cured Meat Stores

You will find speciality stores throughout the country that focus on cheeses and cured meats. These supply a range of ham products, including smoked hams and an amazing variety of cheeses. For an authentic and local experience, visit these stores instead of the supermarket sections selling cheese and cured meats.

Heladerías

Helados is ice cream in Spanish, and Argentines have mastered the art of making it. All over the country you will find artisanal stores as well as well-known chains that can serve you the very best *helados*.

Seafood Stores

With meat and beef dominating the menu in Argentina, it is no surprise that you will not find many dedicated seafood stores, but there are a few gems, particularly along the Atlantic coast. In **Destinations**, you will find a listing of seafood stores by region.

Restaurant Types

No culinary tour would be complete without experiencing the variety of speciality restaurants across Argentina. In **Savor This** you will read about traditional dishes not to miss, and many of these are served best at eateries that specialize in them. Here is a breakdown of the different types of restaurants to seek out, and we'll give you an exhaustive list of specific venues in **Destinations**.

Parrillas

A *parrilla* is a steakhouse, and these are the best places to go for meat cooked on grill. You will have a choice of several cuts of meat to choose from to satisfy any craving for red meat; we detail the different cuts in the *parrilla* section of **Savor This**.

Bodegones

A *bodegon* is a unique type of restaurant that focuses on simple and traditional dishes. You will find *bodegones* mostly in Buenos Aires. These restaurants are not fancy or exclusive, but rather simple and rustic with a keen focus on honest and traditional meals, the kind of meals prepared by "grandmothers." You will not find these restaurants advertised.

There is a growing movement in the country to celebrate *bodegones* and traditional homestyle meals and cooking. This unofficial movement is led by Antigourmet, a group of gourmands in Buenos Aires with an online platform devoted to telling the stories of traditional foods around the city. We had the privilege of interviewing Juan Pablo from the group, and included video clips of this interview on our website. Read more about this movement and recommended *bodegones* at **authenticfoodquest.com/argentinabook**.

Pizzerias

With Italy's large imprint on the food culture in Argentina, **pizzas** are a very popular option. You will find many pizzerias across the country, and they each present a unique Argentine imprint on this casual dish.

Milanesa Restaurants

Milanesa is one of the unique dishes with an Italian heritage that you will find in Argentina. An entry in Savor This describes the dish, and the Destinations section highlights the best places to try *milanesa* for an authentic experience. So important is this one meal that there are restaurants devoted solely to it. Do not miss the chance to try *milanesa* on your travels to Argentina.

Closed Door Restaurants

"Closed door" restaurants, called *puertas cerradas*, are very popular in Buenos Aires and some other major cities. These are basically eating experiences somewhere between a private dinner party and restaurant at the home of a stranger. These are often run by professional chefs who enjoy experimental cooking and creative freedom in an intimate dining experience.

Bar Notables

These are bars with historical and cultural significance in Buenos Aires. There are 73 bars and they are very popular for breakfast and *media tarde* or *merienda*. Stop by one of these bars after a day of sightseeing. Unwind and plunge back into time as you enjoy the historic decor and a *cafe con leche* or artisanal **beer**.

Additional Restaurant Resources

Guía Oleo

To find good restaurants, this app ranks ratings from locals about the price range, neighborhood and cuisine of different restaurants. Think of it as Yelp for Argentina. Price: FREE.

Available for iPhone and Android. http://www.guiaoleo.com.ar

Viajeros

Viajeros is similar to Guía Oleo for restaurants. It also includes hotels and recommendation on what to do in the area.   http://www.viajeros.com

Street Food Vendors

Unlike certain cities in the U.S. or Europe or other South American countries, the street food culture in Argentina is not very developed. You typically will not see people eating on the street or rushing around with coffee mugs. When you find street food, it is generally sold in designated areas rather than at spontaneous "pop-up" booths.

As you get out of the major cities, the street vendors are not as organized. Often times, you will see no signs, just vendors cooking on the street and selling food items. Simply get in line and try something new.

Some of the typical street foods you will find on your trip include *choripán* (grilled sausage), *lomito* (steak sandwich), and *bondiola* (pork shoulder sandwich). See more about the typical and local street foods in Savor This.

Unique Culinary Experiences in Argentina

When it comes to foodie experiences, you will find that Argentina has plenty to offer. Whether you are looking for hands on experiences like cooking classes, or food tours that take you to the best authentic restaurants and stores, you will find all of this and more.

Cooking Classes

Cooking schools and cooking classes are plentiful in Argentina. The majority are concentrated in Buenos Aires, but you will also find some in Mendoza. Learn to make traditional dishes such as *empanadas*, *alfajores*, *locro*, *humitas* and more. Finish off your meals with delicious **Malbec** wines.

You can take group classes or private classes. Some schools also offer classes in English. For vegetarians or travelers with dietary restrictions, many classes will be happy to modify the dishes to accommodate your needs.

Food Tours

If you are short on time and are looking to discover the food in Argentina, consider taking a food tour. Many of the food tours are in Buenos Aires, but you will find some in Mendoza. Food tours are a great way to understand the local specialities, culture and importantly, the flavors.

You will find different options available. You can participate in either group food tours or private food tours. Look for some recommendations in the Buenos Aires and Mendoza sections.

Farm Visits

You will find a few places in Argentina where it is possible to visit farms. In Destinations, you will find detailed information for each region where there are farm visits.

Wine and Beer

You can't go to Argentina without drinking the famous wines from the country: **Malbec** and **Torrontés**. Sure, you can get a great glass of wine at any restaurant in the country, but the best experiences are where the products are produced. We give several recommendations on what to try and where to go in **Savor This** and **Destinations,** including winery and brewery tours and festivals.

Wine Tasting, Mevi Bodega Boutique, Maipú, Mendoza

The two main wine regions in Argentina are Mendoza for the Malbec wines and Cafayate for the famous Torrontés white wines. In **Destinations,** you will find recommendations for wineries to visit.

Argentine culture inherited beer making techniques and celebrations from German and Swiss immigrants in the 19th century. Although **beer** is not the main focus of visitors in Argentina, the making of craft beer is becoming more popular in a few regions.

Here you find a summary of the wine and beer festivals you don't want to miss on your travels to Argentina. Each of these are listed in **Destinations** under their relevant region.

MONTH	WINE & BEER FESTIVAL	REGION
March	**La Fiesta Nacional de la Vendimia** National Harvest Festival	Mendoza
October	**Fiesta de la Picada y la Cerveza Artesanal** Picada and Artisanal Beer Festival	Buenos Aires
October	**Semana del Torrontés** Week of Torrontés	Cafayate
November	**Fiesta Nacional Del Vino Torrontés** National Torrontés Wine Festival	Cafayate
December	**La Semana de la Cerveza Artesanal** Week of Artisanal Beer	Bariloche

Food Festivals

Food is a very important part of Argentine culture and most fairs and festivals feature the local and traditional cuisine. The many towns and villages in the different regions of the country hold local festivals that you want to attend to taste the local specialities.

Listed below is a summary of the major food festivals you want to experience. In the Destinations section, you will find detailed descriptions of the festivals. For additional information about local food festivals in the towns you will be traveling to, visit the local tourist office for events details.

MONTH	FOOD FESTIVAL	REGION
January	**La Fiesta Nacional del Chivo** National Goat Festival	Mendoza
January	**Festival del Queso y la Cabra** Cheese and Goat Festival	Tilcara
February	**Fiesta Nacional del Asado** National Asado Festival	Bariloche
February	**Fiesta Nacional del Curanto** National Curanto Festival	Colonia Suiza
April	**Fiesta Nacional de la Pasta Casera** National Homemade Pasta Festival	Buenos Aires
April	**La Fiesta Nacional del Chocolate** National Chocolate Festival	Bariloche
May	**Feria Masticar** - CHEW Fair	Buenos Aires
July	**Fiesta Nacional del Tamal** National Tamal Festival	Salta
September	**Fiesta Nacional de la Empanada** National Empanada Festival	Salta
September	**Buenos Aires Food Week**	Buenos Aires

MONTH	FOOD FESTIVAL	REGION
September	**Semana de Bodegónes** Week of Bodegónes	Buenos Aires
October	**Raíz Festival de la Gastronomía** Raíz Gastronomy Festival	Buenos Aires
October	**Fiesta Nacional del Pimiento** National Chili Pepper Festival	Cachi
From March to December	**Feria de Mataderos** Mataderos Fair	Buenos Aires

For more information on festivals held throughout Argentina, visit the Fiestas Nacionales website: **FiestasNacionales.org/mapa**

How to Connect and Eat With Locals

With today's technology, eating with locals is much more accessible. Digital apps and platforms allow you to connect with locals around food. Below we highlight three must-have apps for your foodie culinary travels in Argentina.

All these apps connect food lovers to passionate chefs and cooks. They meet up at the home of the host for dinner with locals. You can sign up with each of these apps using your email address or by logging in via Facebook or Twitter.

Choose the dish you wish to eat, book your date, and you are all set for a unique culinary experience. Keep in mind that not all experiences offered on these platforms are authentic Argentine experiences. Choose wisely.

Vizeat
Available for experiences in Buenos Aires, Mendoza, and Cordoba at this time. For more information, check the website: **Vizeat.com**

Eat With
Available for experiences in Buenos Aires only. For more information, check the website: **EatWith.com**

Cook App
Available for experiences in Buenos Aires only. Mendoza, Cordoba, Salta and more are coming soon. For more information, check the website: **CookApp.com**

2. SAVOR THIS
Top Authentic Food & Drinks Not to be Missed on Your Travels

Authentic Specialities

#1: An Authentic Asado
#2: Parrilla
#3: Empanadas
#4: Pasta
#5: Pizza, Fugazetta & Fainá
#6: Milanesa
#7: Tomaticán
#8: Tortitas
#9: Chivito
#10: Locro
#11: Tamales
#12: Humitas
#13: Llama Meat
#14: Trout
#15: Wild Meats: Deer & Wild Boar
#16: Patagonian Lamb
#17: Curanto
#18: Seafood & Fish: King Crab & Patagonian Toothfish

#1: An Authentic Asado

"The asado is an excuse to share the moment, the food, with family and friends. You can cook all the types of meat, sausages and pork and [beef], but more important is with whom you are sharing it."

—Milagros Lorda

The *asado* is considered Argentina's national and most famous dish, but more than a meal, an *asado* is an event that begins in the morning with coaxing a fire to the perfect temperature, then roasting various cuts of beef and other meats on the *parrilla* (grill). As the meal ensues, the cuts come off the grill when they are ready, so that the eaters experience a sequence of courses that lasts for hours.

For any foodie traveler looking to experience authentic food in Argentina, one must experience an *asado*. Besides the food, an *asado* is a social event shared by friends and family to celebrate important moments in life.

The *asado* is closely linked with *gaucho* culture. These South American cattlemen, who are much like the cowboys of North America, mostly live and work the land in the rural Pampas region. Almost every Sunday, family and friends get together over an *asado*.

It begins with the *asador*, who is in charge of the *asado*. While there are regional variations in the grilling process

Asado in San Miguel

such as the type of wood used, the temperature of the grill and distance from the coals, there a few customs that are consistent. The meat is always typically seasoned with only a particular salt that is neither too fine nor too coarse, called *sal parillera*.

The *asado* also typically includes a variety of different cuts of meat, presented in a specific order: *chorizo* (sausage) generally begins the meal, followed by various innards before serving any beef. Ribs are typically brought out first and are then followed by various cuts of beef. Many *asados* will also include chicken, pork, **lamb** and vegetables.

The meat is accompanied by *chimichurri* sauce (see recipe below), and all *asados* include mixed salads, beer and ideally **Malbec** wine.

If the *asador* has gone through all the steps, he typically gets an *aplauso para el asador* which is a traditional round of applause at the end of the meal.

Find a way to get invited to an *asado* on your trip to Argentina. You will not only eat one of the most delicious meals, but you will experience an important part of Argentine culture.

Fun Facts

- Argentina is well known for its beef, and the traditional diet reflects this. At a peak in 1956, the average Argentine ate 100.7 kg (222 lbs) of beef a year. In 2012 the average was down to 58.5 kg (129 lbs).
- Today, Americans eat more beef than Argentines.
- The top 5 countries that eat the most meat (OECD data) are: Australia (205 pounds consumed per person annually), United States (201 pounds), Israel (190 pounds), Argentina (187 pounds), and Uruguay (183 pounds).

Our First Asado in the Pampas

On our quest for authentic food, we had the opportunity to experience an *asado* in Tandil, a little town in the Southern Pampas. We stayed in a private working *estancia* (cattle ranch) called *La Manga*. The asado was organized to celebrate the birthdays of the twelve-year-old daughter and the eighty-six-year-old mother of the farm manager, Santiago Janariz.

The *asado* started in the early afternoon and went into the late hours of the night. Food, wine and conversation flowed easily. Santiago's nieces and nephews are talented musicians and they entertained the group with local folklore songs and dances.

Throughout the evening, people stopped to talk to us about the process and significance of the asado and the romanticized history of the *gaucho*, which we captured on a series of short video clips.

In the videos, you hear the perspective of locals that the gaucho is "more of a mystique than a modern day reality."

Traditional Folklore Music at Asado in Tandil

Video clips:
Visit **authenticfoodquest.com/argentinabook** for more on the *asado* and the gaucho mystique.

Recipes

Learn how to make chimichurri sauce and perfect your own asado at home with the following recipes courtesy of Mirta Rinaldi and the League of Kitchens.

CHIMICHURRI RECIPE

Contrary to what some people think, *chimichurri* never includes cilantro, only parsley. It's a versatile condiment most often served with grilled meats, and may also be used as a marinade. Many Argentines keep a jar in the refrigerator, and as it ages, the vibrant color mellows; it doesn't have to be made fresh at each serving.

Chimichurri sauce

Makes about 1 ⅓ cup
Prep: 5 minutes

- 1 packed cup fresh flat-leaf parsley leaves
- 4 cloves garlic
- 1 tablespoon dried oregano
- 1 tablespoon crushed red pepper flakes
- 1 teaspoon paprika
- 1 teaspoon kosher salt
- 1 teaspoon freshly ground black pepper
- 2 tablespoons balsamic vinegar
- 1 cup extra virgin olive oil

Directions:

Mince the parsley and garlic in a food processor (mini or regular size). Transfer to a medium or large jar with a lid and add the oregano, red pepper flakes, paprika, salt, and pepper. Pour in the vinegar and oil, screw on the lid, and shake well. As the herbs soak in the oil, the sauce will get more flavorful. *Chimichurri* keeps in the refrigerator for about 2 weeks, or 6 months in the freezer.

BEEF SHORT RIBS (COSTILLAS)

Argentina is no doubt synonymous with beef, and *asado*, or barbecue, is practically the national pastime. Double or triple the amount of ribs here to accommodate the size of your party. Offer a salad of lettuce, cherry tomatoes, and rings of white onion dressed with balsamic vinegar and olive oil alongside.

Pork ribs

Directions:

Heat a ridged grill pan over medium-high heat for about 5 minutes until you can hold your hand 3 inches from the surface for only 10 counts. This is how you know it's hot enough.

Salt the ribs very well, about 1/4 teaspoon per side, and place on the grill. When the blood starts to seep through the bone and the meat releases from the

Makes 4 servings
Prep: 10 minutes
Cook: 10 minutes

- 8 flanken-cut beef short ribs, 1-inch thick (about 3 pounds)

Kosher salt, or sal parrillera

Chimichurri (see previous recipe)

grill surface (anywhere from 4 to 6 minutes), flip and cook another 2 to 4 minutes for rare. The grill will smoke a lot but it's ok. Serve with *chimichurri*.

Cook's Note: *Sal parrillera* (similar to kosher salt) is a salt used almost exclusively to salt steak and other meats for grilling. Mirta chooses Dos Anclas brand.

#2: Parrilla
Available everywhere

The smell of grilling meat will greet you when you arrive in Argentina and the many *parrilla* restaurants will tempt you. *Parrilla* is a word that is used interchangeably with *asado*, though it means something different. The

Parrilla at El Desnivel Restaurant, Buenos Aires

word *parrilla* has two meanings. The first refers to an authentic Argentine steakhouse restaurant. The second meaning of *parrilla* is in reference to the actual metal grills that you cook the meat on.

All the *parrillas* offer different experiences, from hole-in-the-wall joints to neighborhood *parrillas,* all the way up to formal and elegant restaurants. Where you choose to go is a personal choice, and once there you will find many choice cuts fresh off the grill.

WHAT TO BEEF ON FROM THE GRILL

Following are some of the most popular cuts of beef you will find in Argentina. This list is not comprehensive, but provides a starting place for any *parrilla*.

Bife de Chorizo (sirloin/ New York strip)

This is your typical mouth-watering Argentine steak. This cut of beef is seared relatively quickly over hot flames. This is the most popular cut and despite its name, it has nothing to do with the *chorizo* sausage.

Lomo / Bife de Lomo (Tenderloin)

This is often the priciest cut on the menu. It is pure and lean meat with very little fat. Although tender and juicy, the lack of fat can sometimes mean lack of flavor. Argentines tend to eat this less as a steak and more as a sandwich called *lomito* (see the street food section).

Ojo de Bife (Ribeye)

This classic is found at practically every *parrilla* in the country. It is one of the best cuts of meat from the rib section of the cow. One of its characteristics is the marbling of fat which results in great flavors. Don't miss this cut at a *parrilla*.

Bife de Chorizo at El Desnivel

Vacío (Flank steak)

This is an interesting cut, and not one that's often served outside of Argentina/Uruguay. It is a popular cut for **asados**. It is known for its juicy underside, covered by a thick layer of fat on top that gets crispy as the cut is cooked. *Vacío* is a mix of muscle groups named for the "empty space" that surrounds the stomach area.

Entraña (Skirt steak)

When looking for something more manageable than a full size *lomo* or *bife de chorizo,* try the skirt steak. This is another Argentine favorite cut of meat. It is quite flavorful, though not as tender. Be prepared to chew a little more.

HOW TO ORDER YOUR BEEF

Argentines tend to like their beef well done, or *bien cocinado*. If you want to specify how you want your meat cooked, get to know these handy terms below:

"Blue" (very rare) — just say *vuelta y vuelta* which means very quickly cooked on each side
Juguso — rare
Medio-juguso — medium rare
Punto — medium
Bien Cocinado — well done

> **TIP:** Steak servings at restaurants are typically quite large. Be prepared to share.

WHAT ELSE IS ON THE GRILL

Beyond the meat, try these staples that you will find at a *parrilla*:

Provoleta

Provoleta is a type of cheese that you could say is a distant relative of Provolone cheese. It is usually grilled alongside the meat. It is crispy and slightly caramelized on the outside and gooey on the inside. It is doused in olive oil, served with tomatoes and is really good. Don't miss out on experiencing *provoleta* at a *parrilla*.

Sausages and Offal

Chorizo — pork sausages (fresh sausages that look like Italian sausages with paprika or peppers)

Morcilla — blood sausages (very tasty with a soft mushy texture)

If you are feeling adventurous try the following organ meats or offal:

Mollejas — sweetbreads (smooth and tender with an exquisite and mild flavor)

Chinchulín — intestines (chewy in texture with subtle flavors)

Riñones — kidneys (tender muscle meat with outstanding flavors)

> To learn more about cooking with fire, get your hands on **Seven Fires: Grilling the Argentine Way**, by chef and author Francis Mallmann.

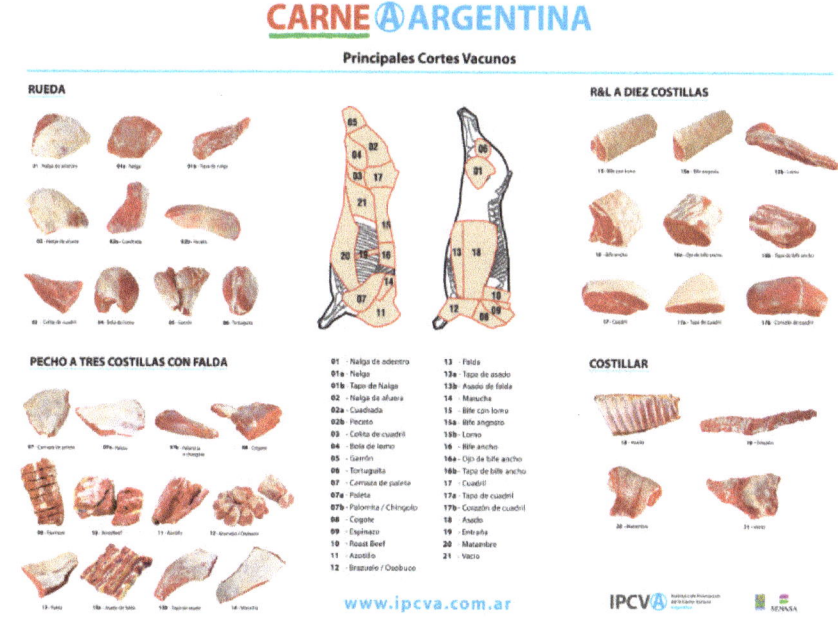

Source: www.ipcva.com.ar

Plates of Empanadas

#3: Empanadas

Available everywhere with regional differences; available vegetarian

Empanadas are another quintessentially Argentine dish; you could follow in our culinary footsteps and tour the different regions of Argentina simply by indulging in these savory treats. *Empanada* literally means "wrapped in bread," and these small savory pies are filled with a variety of ingredients.

Throughout Argentina we found the typical *carne* (ground beef), *picante carne* (spicy ground beef), *pollo* (chicken) and *jamon y queso* (ham and cheese), but we also found more unique variations like **llama**, sweet squash, and a delicious sweet corn filling called **humitas**. Vegetarians will be pleased with the many non-meat options such as *queso y cebolla* (cheese and onion) and *espinaca* (spinach).

Argentine *empanadas* are considered to be some of the best in the world for the cooking and regional differences. *Empanadas* have a semi-circular shape, not exceeding 20 cm (8 in) in diameter. The seal of the wrap, called the *repulgue* is done by hand or with a fork, and this is a distinctive element: the type of close or fold is an indicator of the ingredients used in the filling. Some are elegantly twisted, some are dimpled in distinct patterns, and each closure serves as a code for the filling inside.

You can eat *empanadas* anytime. Grab them to go as a snack or buy a dozen and make a whole meal out of the experience.

DIFFERENT TYPES OF EMPANADAS

Most Argentines will agree that the best *empanadas* come from the north of Argentina. The two most popular types of *empanadas* you will hear about are *empanadas salteñas* from the Salta Province and *empanadas* from Tucuman.

Empanada Salteñas

Empanadas salteñas tend to be slightly smaller in size and are baked in the clay ovens. Our favorite and a favorite of many are the *carne* or beef *empanadas*. They are deliciously prepared with green onion and potatoes. They are often accompanied by a red spicy sauce. Try them at **La Casa de las Empanadas**, the "House of Empanadas" in Cafayate (see **Destinations, Cafayate**).

Empanadas from Tucumán

Empanadas Salteñas

The love for *empanadas* runs deep in Tucumán in the north of Argentina. There is even a National Empanada Festival that is held there every September. At the tourism office you can pick up the Ruta de la Empanada ("*empanada* route"), a guide to find the best *empanadas* in every neighborhood across the province.

In Tucuman, the traditional fillings for *empanadas* are more limited. You will find beef, chicken and one of the most authentic is *mondongo* or tripe. In Tucuman, the *empanadas* do not have potatoes and the meat is chopped and cooked with green onions, cumin, red and white pepper, paprika and garlic. The *empanadas* are cooked in a clay oven or fried.

Empanadas from The North of Argentina: Jujuy Province

Argentine food in the North of Argentina is influenced by the indigenous Andean culture that extends through the neighboring countries of Bolivia and Paraguay. Unlike the Italian and Spanish influence you find in Buenos Aires, the food of northern Argentina incorporates crops native to the region.

When it comes to the *empanadas* from the north, you will find local specialities like *empanadas* filled with **llama** meat and **quinoa**. Take the time to appreciate these *empanadas* on your travels. Enjoy the unique llama *empanadas* and the subtle, hearty flavors of the quinoa *empanadas*.

Quinoa Empanada

Empanadas from Mendoza

Mendoza, Argentina's beautiful wine country also has their own unique twist on *empanadas*. The traditional *Mendocini empanadas* use beef, onions, hard boiled eggs and green olives. Mendoza-style *empanadas* are always baked and never fried. Once baked to perfection, enjoy these delicacies with the region's famous Malbec wines.

> Visit **authenticfoodquest.com/argentinabook** to view a short video with Chef Matias cooking Mendocini *empanadas* at **Siete Fuegos**, a Francis Mallmann Restaurant at The Vines Resort & Spa, Mendoza. See more in *Destinations*.

Patagonia Empanadas

Empanadas are also popular in the south of Argentina. Influenced by a variety of natural resources, you will find *empanadas* filled with Patagonian lamb, or seafood: mussels and king crab are some of the specialities of the area. Be sure to taste Argentina through its diverse *empanadas* on your travels.

To read further about our discovery of Argentina through its emblematic *empanadas,* check out the following article "Discovering Argentina through Empanadas" at **authenticfoodquest.com/argentinabook**.

Empanadas al horno de barro

HOW TO EAT EMPANADAS LIKE AN ARGENTINE

Tips From Top Chef, Francis Mallmann

We sat down with Argentine top chef, Francis Mallmann at his restaurant Patagonia Sur in Buenos Aires and we discovered that there is in fact a technique to eating *empanadas*.

If you would like to eat *empanadas* like an Argentine, apply these 3 tips shared by Francis Mallmann.

1. First you don't want to use a fork and knife. It is a sacrilegious. An *empanada* is to be eaten with your hands to appreciate it to its best.

2. Second, when you bite your *empanada*, you don't want to let anything fall on your plate. You want to show that you really enjoy the *empanada*, which means nothing is to be omitted. However, that presents a dilemma. The *empanadas* come from the *horno* (clay oven) hot and you are almost sure to burn yourself. It takes skill, delicacy and patience to apply this particular tip.

3. Third, you want to get your *empanada* cooked in the *horno de barro* (clay oven). These are said to be the best. To make sure that the *empanadas* were cooked in an *horno de barro*, you will notice that the dough of the *empanada* "bubbles" up at the surface. This is a signature of a "real" *empanada*.

#4: Pasta

Available everywhere, available vegetarian

The Italian influence in Argentina runs deep and is especially evident in the food. As noted earlier, Italians immigrated into Argentina in the 19th and 20th centuries, ultimately forming one of the most powerful immigrant communities in the country. Some say that roughly 60% of Argentines have at least one drop of Italian blood running through their veins. The largest concentration is in Buenos Aires and in the neighborhoods of La Boca and San Telmo.

With so many European immigrants moving to Argentina, it became one of the first countries in South America to develop a local pasta industry in the 1880s and 1890s. Sunday dinner in Argentina is one of the most significant meals of the week. The meal often includes **asado** and/or pasta. You will notice a fascination for fresh and stuffed pasta in the sheer number of pasta speciality stores in the neighborhoods.

Fresh pasta

Your culinary adventure through Argentina will not be complete without eating pasta. You will find many stores selling *pasta artesanales* everywhere. The variety of noodles (*fideos*) is huge: linguini, gnocchi, cannelloni and the most sought after, the **raviol** (ravioli). Unique Argentine specialities like the cheese-stuffed **sorrentinos** are popular.

In general, pasta is sold by the kilo at very affordable prices. You will also find a wide range of sauces available from *bolonesa*, and *cuatro quesos* (four cheeses), to pesto with lots of basil and olive oil, and tomato-based sauces made with eggplants, tomatoes, garlic, salt and olive oil.

The raviolis are sold by the box or by the *plancha* (which means the board). A serving of about 48 individual *raviol* is more than enough for two people. The fresh pasta takes no more than five minutes to cook, but do ask because cooking time changes depending on the type of pasta.

Argentina Ñoquis (Gnocchi)

Argentines consider the 29th of each month as the *Dia de Ñoquis*—the Day of Gnocchi. On this day everyone gets together to eat (though no one accurately remembers the reason why). The folk origin of this tradition claims that the 29th of each month was just before people got paid on the first, and with money tight they only had potatoes and flour left to eat. Gnocchi, or *ñoquis* were born as the perfect solution as they are filling and not expensive.

These little dumplings made from potato and flour are traditionally served in tomato sauce. They are an easy and economical dish to make.

There are a number of other stories of how this tradition got started. Italian immigrants are said to have brought this tradition with them. Some say that the 29th was the day when the Italian Saint Pantaleo was canonized, and the tradition of the 29th honors him and the miracles attributed to him. Regardless of the reason, the *Dia de Ñoquis* is a fun and frequent celebration.

Ñoquis

Traditionally, money is placed under the plate at dinner to attract luck and prosperity. Everyone at the table gets to keep the money for luck. Some say you have to donate that money to charity in order to get good fortune. With this tradition, on this day you'll see many restaurants, supermarkets and pasta shops offering *ñoquis* specials.

Sorrentinos Pasta: An Argentine Specialty

The *sorrentino* pasta is one of the best known and popular kinds of pasta in Argentina. They are larger than *raviol* and more rounded. They are usually stuffed with ham and various cheeses (mozzarella, ricotta, etc.). You can also find vegetarian fillings like pumpkin and spinach.

The origin of this popular Argentine pasta is uncertain. It is said to have been created by the chef and restaurant owner of a mythical restaurant called Sorrento, located in Buenos Aires. He decided to create a new larger breed of ravioli that would be different. This type of pasta is typical to Argentina and one that you would not find in Italy.

Sorrentinos

In **Destinations**, we have highlighted pasta stores that are authentic and recommended to us. Don't hesitate to ask locals, as you will find them to have strong opinions about the pasta and where to purchase it.

Fun Facts Pasta

- The busiest time for buying fresh pasta is around midday. You will find long lines with people patiently waiting in line for their pasta. Pasta stores often run out, so plan on getting there early to get your favorite choice.

- In Argentina, a *ñoqui* (gnocchi) is a person who is legally registered as a worker, usually for the government, and receives a monthly wage, but who performs little or no work. Perhaps this connects to the origin story of the *Dia de Ñoquis*, or perhaps it is the shape of the doughy dumplings that helps give the word its double meaning.

- Pasta, along with *parrillas* and pizza, are the "Holy Trinity" of the Buenos Aires cuisine.

#5: Pizza, Fugazetta & Fainá
Buenos Aires and around, available vegetarian

Some say that Buenos Aires has more pizzerias than Rome. Whether that's true or not, pizza certainly holds a cherished place of importance in Argentina, and like other dishes with European roots, Argentines have given pizza a new flair of their own.

Fugazetta

Pizza is so important that in 2007, the Ministry of Culture of Buenos Aires released their gastronomy guide called "**Pizzerías de Valor Patrimonial de Buenos Aires,**" highlighting 39 remarkable pizzerias in the city. The BBC reported in 2011 that pizza is overtaking steak as the most popular dish for diners in Argentina.

Before you assume you know everything about what pizza looks and tastes like, first experience the unique pizza of Buenos Aires. Pizza in Argentina is different in two significant ways. First, pizza in Argentina uses very little tomato sauce. Secondly, Argentines use an ungodly amount of cheese on their pizza; Argentines are said to use three times more cheese on their pizzas than Italians.

The most unique type of pizza you will find in Argentina is the *fugazetta*. This Buenos Aires classic has been listed by the Argentine government as

Argentine Pizza Tips

The major types of pizza you will find on your travels are:

- ***Pizza al molde*** is a thick spongy doughy pizza about 1 inch or 2cm thick
- ***Media masa***, half baked, is commonly found at supermarkets as pre-cooked dough to be finished in the oven at home
- ***Pizza a la piedra*** is a thin crust pizza
- ***Pizza a la parrilla*** is thin crust pizza cooked on the parrilla (grill)

Pizza eaten by the slice to go is called ***pizza al corte*** or ***pizza al paso***. You can more about this in the street food section.

It is not unusual to see locals eating pizza standing up accompanied by beer or moscato wine and ***fainá***.

foods under "Patrimonial Value." This thick crust pizza is stuffed with mozzarella, and topped with onions and even more cheese, and served with a splash of olive oil and oregano.

It was invented at **Banchero** (see Destinations, Buenos Aires), a restaurant you can still visit in the colorful La Boca neighborhood. It dates back to 1893, when Don Agustin Banchero arrived from Genoa, Italy to try his luck in Buenos Aires. He started a little bakery with his son Juan, becoming the first pizza joint in the city. One day as the story goes, his son added cheese to the traditional dough to keep it from drying out and as a result invented what became the sauceless *fugazetta con queso*.

Fainá

Fainá is a very popular accompaniment to pizza in Argentina. It is a thin bread, gluten free, made from chickpeas. The simple ingredients are chickpea flour, water, oil and salt.

Fainá is served in slices alongside your pizza. It is moist inside and crunchy on the outside.

Don't be surprised at the way Argentines eat *fainá*. It can be eaten alone, or placed on top of the pizza, adding more dimension to the already thick pizza. When eaten on top of the pizza it is known as *pizza a la caballo* (horseback pizza).

Fainá came to Argentina with the wave of Italian immigrants from the 19th and 20th centuries. *Fainá* still exists in Liguria, Italy where it is known as *farinata*, its name in Genovese dialect.

Fainá

Fun Facts About Fainá:

There are similar variations with different names that can found all over the world.

- *Socca* in Italy
- *Farinata* in Tuscany
- *Besan* in South Asia
- *Pudla* in India

#6: Milanesa
Available everywhere

Milanesa

The Italian-fusion dish *milanesa* is so wildly popular that it has become an Argentine national dish. Its fame is not limited to Argentina; you can find it in countries across South America.

Crispy and savory, *milanesa* is a thin cut of protein (usually beef, but it's also made with chicken, veal, cod fish, and even vegetarian options in soy or quinoa) dipped in eggs, covered with breadcrumbs, and then fried in oil. *Milanesa* is normally served with a plate of fries, mashed potatoes or salad.

But one variation, the *Milanesa a la Napolitana*, is the subject of pop legend. On the night of its invention in the 1940s, the story goes, a customer waltzed into El Nápolitano just as the famous restaurant was closing up in Buenos Aires. He asked for a *milanesa*. The cook, in a tired rush, burned one side, and as he agonized over how to save the dish, the owner suggested they cover the *milanesa* with tomato sauce, ham, and mozzarella cheese, and let it melt.

Thus, the crispy-gooey *Milanesa a la Napolitana* was born. The customer loved it so much, it became a regular menu item. A less dramatic but probably more true version of the story claims that the dish was invented deliberately to be inserted into the menu.

Regardless of how this dish came to be, the *Napolitana* variation is now a dish you can find all across Argentina. For a lunchtime special, *milanesa* is often served as a sandwich; read more about the ***sándwich de milanesa*** in the Street Food section.

Stop in the **Club de la Milanesa** (see Destinations, Buenos Aires) to try a selection of over 20 different *milanesa* sandwiches, or visit the **Mercado del Progreso** (Destinations) in Buenos Aires to watch live demonstrations of *milanesa* being made.

So important is this dish that it has been listed by the Argentina government as foods under "patrimonial value". Any traveller wishing to experience the heritage of Argentina must try it.

Tomaticán

#7: Tomaticán
A Mendoza speciality, vegetarian

Tomaticán is a simple tomato-based dish that highlights the flourishing food scene in Mendoza, a lush farming area at the foot of the Andes. Similar in consistency to tomato soup, it starts with ripe farm-grown tomatoes topped with green onions, oregano, breadcrumbs, and sometimes an egg. This dish is typically eaten at home and each family has their own unique variation of the *tomaticán*.

When it comes to the local produce, Mendoza is known for its fruits (pears, apples, peaches in the summer), vegetables (tomatoes, potatoes, carrots, zucchini) olives and olive oils. Together with goat meat, lamb and beef, these ingredients converge into a distinctive culinary identity.

The tomato is one of the most celebrated vegetables in Mendoza. The variations in temperatures, along with the altitude concentrate the flavors of the tomatoes giving them a deep rich color and intense flavors. In addition to fresh tomatoes, dried tomatoes are also really popular and just as delicious.

Fun Facts

- Mendoza is the main tomato growing region in Argentina, as well as a producer of olive oil and wine; you can visit farms and wineries while you are there.

- About 70 km (43 mi) from downtown Mendoza is home to Argentina's most popular mineral water, Villavicencio. Try this great tasting water and take a tour of the Villavicencio Natural Reserve. See the **Destinations** for more details.

If you are looking to splurge ask the tourist office for a round-up of Mendoza's more expensive eateries called the *Guía Mendoza Gourmet*.

TOMATICÁN AT NUTRI VERDE VEGETARIANO RESTAURANT, MENDOZA

At the time of our visit to Mendoza, the only restaurant that we could find serving *tomaticán* was Nutri Verde Vegetariano (a great vegetarian restaurant option). The restaurant did not actually have *tomaticán* on the menu, but they made it specially for us once we told them about our quest to discover this local *Mendocini* speciality.

We found this dish surprisingly sweet from the tomatoes. From a texture perspective, we found it a little mushy—not quite a soup but not enough consistency to chew on. Overall, the dish was wonderful and delicious and something you don't want to miss on your visit to Mendoza.

> Visit **authenticfoodquest.com/argentinabook** to watch a short video of owner and cook at Nutri Verde Vegetariano explaining how she makes *Tomaticán*.

*Maria Antonieta offers *tomaticán*, though it is not a staple but a seasonal dish. Vanina Chimeno puts her unique twist on it by making it more like a soup and adding green beans and other seasonal ingredients.

An Interview with Chef Vanina Chimeno, Mariá Antoneita Restaurant, Mendoza

To understand the local and authentic specialities in Mendoza, we sat down with chef and owner, Vanina Chimeno of the popular Mariá Antoneita restaurant in Mendoza (see Destinations, Mendoza for more on the restaurant).

In a short video, Vanina Chimeno discusses what makes the produce in Mendoza exceptional. From her point of view, the fruits and vegetables are exceptional due to the variation in the weather. It is typically very hot in the day and freezing cold at night, and this concentrates the flavors of the produce, making them succulent and delicious.

We also had the chance to discuss the future of Argentine cooking. In another short video, Vanina Chimeno shares her thoughts on the future of Argentine cooking. She believes that in Argentina today, there is a movement taking place to honor and celebrate Argentine recipes and cooking culture.

> To watch both videos (and more) visit
> **authenticfoodquest.com/argentinabook**

#8: Tortitas

A Mendoza speciality, vegetarian

Tortitas: Pinchada, Manteca, Hoja

Tortitas are small little pastries that are traditional from Mendoza. These simple pastries are made with just a few ingredients: water, flour, butter, yeast and salt. You will find them sold inexpensively at *panaderías* (bakeries).

These versatile pastries can be eaten at any time of the day. They are often made at home and eaten for breakfast. They go well with coffee or **mate** and can be enjoyed with honey, marmalade or **dulce de leche**.

There are three main kinds of *tortitas*. The one thing they all have in common is copious amounts of butter. They are delicious, but be careful of eating too many.

BONUS TIP

Tortitas are the perfect snack to carry with you in between winery visits. These little bites will fill you up and soak in the alcohol as you prepare for your next wine tasting. Don't miss out on these little pastries; you will be surprised how many ways you will find to enjoy them

---

#9: Chivito

A Mendoza speciality

Chivito is grilled meat of a young goat eaten in the country, often as part of an *asado*. This young goat is no longer in the suckling stage, but not reached adulthood yet. The *chivito* is less gamey and tends to have a more delicate flavor than an adult goat.

Chivito can be cooked *a la parrilla* (grilled) or *a la cruz*. In the case of *chivito a la cruz*, the *chivito* is fastened onto a cross which is nailed to the ground near a fire, which then gives the goat a special flavor.

Every year there is a **Chivito Festival** that is held in the town of Malargüe in the province of Mendoza. Read more about this festival in Destinations, Mendoza, where the main attraction is the goats cooking on open fires.

When in the Mendoza region, be sure to try a *chivito* meal or a *chivito* sandwich.

> ### GOOD TO KNOW
>
> A younger goat called *cabrito* is another regional speciality from Córdoba Province in Argentina. Unlike the *chivito* which is old enough to eat solid foods, the *cabrito* is still at the suckling stage. There is a festival dedicated to the *Cabrito* called *Festival del Cabrito* that takes place in January, outside of Cordoba in the town of Quilino.

#10: Locro
Andean Northwest Region

The northwest region of Argentina is distinctly different from Buenos Aires. Set against the Andes Mountains, you will appreciate the dry and unusual landscape with its fascinating colors and formations.

Locro Pulsado

This is where you will find *locro*, a hearty stew made with beans, corn, squash, and onions, with bay leaf and cumin for seasoning and a meat that varies by region and family recipe: it is sometimes beef, pork, or *chorizo* (the traditional Argentine sausage).

Its name, *ruqru* or *Iugru*, comes from the Incan language, *Quechua*. The vast majority of the population along the Andes range are of native Inca descent. The native language of *Quechua* is spoken and there is a definite Andean feel with llamas, traditional crafts, indigenous communities and Inca ruins.

The food in this region draws heavily on the indigenous culture. *Locro* is one of the most classic traditional dishes from this region.

Locro is the main dish associated with the independence of Argentina. It is known to some as the national dish of the country. Every 25th of May, Argentines celebrate the May Revolution in 1810 that led to the country's independence from Spain in 1816. The extended family gets together to share a meal and celebrate. It is also the perfect dish for the colder autumn and winter days.

There are several different ways to prepare *locro*. One popular style is *locro pulsado*.

This particular variation has beef, white beans, white corn, green onions, chorizo, paprika, cumin pepper and salt.

Don't hesitate to try out *Locro* on your travels to Argentina. You will enjoy the hearty flavors of this belly warming dish.

Read more about our experience finding *locro* at **authenticfoodquest.com/argentinabook**. In our article, "Discovering 3 Typical Dishes from Salta," we took an 18-hour bus ride and two failed attempts before we finally got to taste this hearty soup.

> **Facts About Locro**
>
> - Locro can also be found in Ecuador, Colombia and Peru. Each country interprets the recipe differently—adding vegetables, using different meats and cuts and changing up the spices.
> - While there are variations on the different types of meat used, organ meat like tripe and intestines are popular as well as pigs' feet.

#11: Tamales
Andean Northwest Region

Tamales are one of the most popular regional dishes of the northwest region of Argentina, particularly in the provinces of Jujuy, Salta, Catamarca and Tucumán. The *tamales* here are nothing like the Mexican *tamales* you find in the US. *Tamales* in this region are referred to as *tamales salteños*.

The *tamales* are wrapped in corn husks and tied up to look like a "bonbon." A delicious corn based dough (*masa*) forms the base. The filling used in *tamales salteños* is ground beef, potatoes, spices (*ají*) and salt and pepper.

You will enjoy these incredibly delicious *tamales*; the combination of the corn, beef and the various spices is heavenly. Be prepared for these to become one of your favorites from the Andean Northwest region. Note that each region will prepare them a little differently, so be sure to get the *tamales salteños*.

Tamales: wrapped, open, cut in half

#12: Humitas
Andean Northwest Region, vegetarian

Humitas in corn husks (salty version)

Another popular and indigenous dish from the Andes is the *humita*. This dish is also popular in Peru, Bolivia and Chile. The word "humita" comes from *"jumint'a"*, the name given by the Quechua people to a sweet corn bun wrapped in corn husks and cooked in water.

There are two main preparation methods for *humitas*: *humitas a la olla* (sweet corn buns in a pot or stew) and *humitas y en chala* which are cooked in corn husks. Each region has its own speciality, and you can find *humitas* in sweet and salty varieties.

In Mendoza for example, you will find sweet *humitas* made with sweet corn, onions, milk, butter and chili flakes. Further north, you will find the salty version. These are the very popular *humitas en chala*. On the inside you will find a sweet corn filling with goat cheese (regional speciality) and *picante* (spicy) seasoning.

The secret to a good *humita* is to use corn that is picked when it is very ripe (*cau* or *choclero*), but not dry. They are always wrapped in fresh corn husks to intensify the flavor. Closer to the Amazon you can find *humitas* made with yuca or plantains instead of corn.

If you are a corn lover, you will be in heaven. Once you unwrap the corn husks and take your first bite, the combination of salty and sweet, mixed with the gooey cheese will simply melt in your mouth.

#13: Llama Meat
Andean Northwest Region

One of the striking images you will see in the north of Argentina are llamas roaming freely. For more than 3,000 years, the people of the Andes used llamas to transport goods. Llama meat was also their primary source of meat.

Today, llama meat is eaten widely in the northwest part of Argentina. The meat is low in fat, high in protein and fiber which helps keep cholesterol levels down. The health benefits make this meat worth trying on your travels.

For a snack, you will find llama meat sold as dried meat (similar to beef jerky) called *salame de llama*. At restaurants, the two most common llama preparations you will find are *cazuela de llama* and *lomo de llama*.

The *cazuela de llama* is typically slow cooked and prepared as a stew, similar to the preparation of a French "boeuf bourguignon."

Llama

Native potatoes, carrots and rice are popular accompaniments. The *lomo de llama* is similar to a steak of llama meat. Thin slices of llama meat are pan fried and served with native potatoes.

If you have never had llama meat before, try it in the northwest of Argentina where it is a local and authentic speciality. Pair it with a fine glass of Malbec wine or artisanal beer from the region.

Cazuela de Llama (top),
Lomo de Llama (bottom)

Fun Facts About Llamas

- Most llamas typically do not spit on people, unless they are provoked. Approach them gently.
- Llama meat is mainly produced in Argentina and Chile.
- Sweaters and socks made from llama fur are warm and soft with a luxurious feel.

#14: Trout
Patagonia and The Lake Region

Bariloche is the principal destination in the Lake Region. It is surrounded by mountains, rivers, forests, lakes and dominated by the Andean Mountain Range. Here, you will find a strong influence of the early German and Swiss settlers. This comes through in the architecture as well as the regional cuisine.

The gastronomy options in Bariloche are varied. You will find the classics such as **asado**, homemade pasta and pizza. For local and authentic specialities try out the regional delicacies, which include trout, deer, Patagonia lamb, wild boar and *curanto* (a feast of seafood and meats steamed among hot stones).

Trout or Trucha

The local fish speciality you don't want to miss is the trout or *trucha* (in Spanish). You will see many local restaurants selling trout cooked in creamy sauces, mixed with pasta or pan fried.

The best way to enjoy the delicious texture and taste of the trout, is to have it *al natural* and simply prepared over a **parrilla**. Skip the sauces and taste the real flavors of one of the authentic and regional delicacies. See Destinations for recommended restaurant options.

Smoked Trout or Trucha Ahumada

Typical of this region and from the European immigrant heritage, you will also find smoked local specialities, including smoked wild meats, salmon, trout and more.

In keeping with the trout speciality, do make it a point to also try smoked trout. Familia Weiss, founded by Ernesto Weiss, an Austrian who settled in the Bariloche in the 1960s founded a smokehouse that bears his name. You will find these products in Bariloche and across the country.

Grilled Trout   Smoked Trout

Trout Farm Visit

To better appreciate the trout in Bariloche, visit a trout farm. Pisciculture (fish breeding) is practiced in this region as part of sustainable resource management to protect wild trout populations. Visit **Criadero Truchas Colonia Suiza** (see **Destinations**), a fantastic trout farm just outside of Bariloche.

> ### VIDEO - THE DISAPPEARING TROUT
>
> In an interview with Matias Bollinger, the chef and owner of Alto El Fuego Parrilla, we learned that restaurants are not allowed to sell wild trout; only farm raised trout is served. According to Chef Matias, this is due to two factors. First, to preserve the wild trout. And secondly, to maintain Bariloche's popularity as a fly fishing destination. Even so, in some areas fishermen can only catch one trout per person per day.
>
> See more at **authenticfoodquest.com/argentinabook**

#15: Wild Meats: Deer & Wild Boar
Patagonia and The Lake Region

The meat specialities in Bariloche also include *ciervo* (deer) and *jabali* (wild boar). These wild meats are best enjoyed in the winter months, but you will find them in Bariloche year round.

Deer (Ciervo)

Ciervo is typically prepared as a stew or goulash mostly in the winter months. You will generally not find it available as slices like a steak, because the meat is too tough and not tender enough.

Another popular way which *ciervo* is prepared is as an *escabeche de ciervo*. This is marinated deer or pickled deer in oil and vinegar. You will enjoy the tangy flavors and delicious combinations of vinegar, onions, carrots and cloves.

Deer (Escabeche de Ciervo) (top), Wild Boar (Jabali) (bottom)

Wild Boar (Jabali)

Jabali or wild boar is the other local speciality of the area. You will find it available in different preparation styles based on the season. At the time of our visit to Bariloche, we had it served on a platter in the form of thin slices. This surprising presentation was deliciously rewarding. The meat was full of deep and intense strong flavors.

If you have never had wild boar before, don't hesitate to try this local speciality in Bariloche.

#16: Patagonian Lamb
Patagonia and The Lake Region

In Calafate, your order of savory *cordero* (lamb) will come with Calafate berries–small bright barberries that complement the meat. Legend has it that if you eat a Calafate berry, you are destined to return to Patagonia. This might have less to do with your fate and more to do with how much you will fall in love with the local food culture.

Patagonian Lamb

Cordero, Patagonian lamb, is the local delicacy of this region. You will find it in Bariloche, El Calafate and all the way south to Ushuaia. Lamb is native here, and has been used as a food source since the earliest indigenous Mapuche Indians.

The Patagonian lamb is one of the most prized meats in Argentina. The lamb is typically free range and grass fed in the Patagonian steppe. You will see lambs roaming freely on your drive around Patagonia. The meat is quite lean and the lamb from Patagonia does not have the strong flavor notes that can be found in other lambs around the world.

Meat is harvested seasonally, and *cordero* is best enjoyed December through April. After that period, the lamb you will find available will most likely be frozen.

Patagonia lamb is a registered trademark and carries a logo for geographical indication: the CORDERO PATAGÓNICO. This logo is used to show the specific area of the country where the lamb comes from, the way the lambs are raised, and their unique taste that comes from grazing a variety of pastures.

In Patagonia, the best way to enjoy *cordero* is to simply have it cooked on the *parrilla*. Skip all the other different types of preparation styles and enjoy the natural flavors of lamb cooked simply and on the grill.

Curanto at Restaurante Victor Goye

#17: Curanto
Patagonia and The Lake Region

The word *curanto* means "hot rock," and before you eat this delicious meal of slow roasted and smoked meats and vegetables, you must see the ceremony by which it is prepared.

A *curanto* is the traditional food of the Mapuche, who are a group of indigenous people of Southern Chile and Southwestern Argentina, including Patagonia. Today you will find this tradition in *Colonia Suiza* (Swiss Colony) just outside of Bariloche.

The ceremony begins with a shallow hole dug in the ground, about 15 cm (6 in) deep. The hole is lined with thin *coihue* branches, and the branches are covered with rocks. A fire is lit. When the wood is burned, the hot rocks fall to the bottom of the hole.

Once this happens, the rocks are covered with maqui or nalca leaves (local bushes). Beef, lamb, pork, chicken, sausages, potatoes, sweet potatoes, apples, onions, carrots and squash are then placed on the leaves and covered again with another layer of maqui leaves. Dirt is poured over the shallow hole and everything is left to cook for at least three hours.

When the cooking is done, smoke starts to emerge from the ground indicating that the curanto is ready. The food is cooked tenderly by the heat of the stones and has a delicious slightly smoky flavor.

More than a meal, a *curanto* is an experience. Make a reservation at **Restaurante Victor Goye** (see Destinations) in *Colonia Suiza* to see this unique tradition.

#18: Seafood & Fish: King Crab & Patagonian Toothfish
Patagonia and The Lake Region

Located in the southernmost tip of South America is Ushuaia, the capital of Tierra del Fuego. This busy port is on the Beagle Channel and a popular gateway city to the Antarctic Continent and the South Pole. It is nicknamed

Southern King Crab

El Fin del Mundo, the End of the World.

Food from the *Tierra del Fuego* (Fuegian food) is influenced heavily by the natural resources. Fresh fish and seafood comes from the South Atlantic and Beagle Channel. The specialities of the region include Southern king crab (*centolla*), sea bass (*merluza negra*), large mussels (*cholgas*), and octopus. *Centolla* or Southern King crab is one of the most popular specialities.

Eating at the "end of the world" is an experience. You will find plenty of restaurant options on the main street, Avenue San Martin. Most of these restaurants will offer familiar options such as pizza, pasta, and pastries. Since you will have made it this far to the southernmost city in the world, it is worth getting off the beaten path and experiencing the local and authentic specialities.

Southern King Crab (Centolla)

This is the signature dish in Ushuaia and one you should plan on indulging in on your trip. The crab comes from Cape Horn and you will find many restaurants offering it in Ushuaia. The meat is tender and resembles that of Alaskan King crab, though sweeter and meatier.

When you order it, avoid the restaurants that douse it in a thick sauce. Be sure to order it "naked" and devoid of any sauces, except a slice of lemon. Give yourself a chance to taste the unique and subtle flavors of this particular crab.

Patagonian Toothfish (Merluza Negra)

This fish is actually known as Patagonian Toothfish. It is found in the deep waters, between 300 and 3,500 meters (1,000 to 11,400 feet), and is found on the continental shelves of most sub-Antarctic islands.

This fish is also sold under the trade names of Chilean Seabass in the USA and Canada; *merluza negra* in Argentina, Peru and Uruguay; and *mero* in Japan and Spain.

Patagonian Toothfish

Ordering this fish from the deep waters of Antarctica should be a must on your trip to Ushuaia. Savor and enjoy the fine and delicate flavors of this white fish.

In the picture above, this fish is prepared *en papillote* (French for "in parchment"), accompanied with julienne cut leeks and carrots. The sauce is fine, light and very tasty.

Street Food

#1: Choripán
#2: Lomito
#3: Milanesa Sandwich
#4: Pancho
#5: Sandwich de Miga and Tostadas
#6: Bondiola
#7: Tortilla
#8: Pizza by the Slice
#9: Empanadas
#10: Garrapiñadas

While street food in Argentina is not as developed as in other Latin countries, you can still get something to eat on the go. However, most street food vendors in Argentina typically have plastic chairs and tables allowing you to take the time and eat. Even though it is "fast food", the Argentine culture around food calls for taking the time to enjoy and savor the flavors.

Street Food Vendor at Costanera Sur, Buenos Aires

Minutas are local Argentine fast foods. These are dishes that are simple and quick to prepare. The tradition of *minutas* was invented to offer affordable food to the working people. The most popular *minutas* are **milanesa**, **empanadas** and pizza by the slice.

On your travels through Argentina, eat at least once on the street, pick from any of the street foods in this section and enjoy Argentina-style street food.

#1: Choripán
Available everywhere
Affectionately called the *chori*, this is the street food of choice for many Argentines. This fast food is basically a sausage, made of 70% beef and 30% pork, cooked on a grill and served between two pieces of bread.

Choripán

The *choripán* is usually seasoned with **chimichurri** sauce made from oregano, parsley, garlic, chili flakes and red wine vinegar.

Choris are traditionally eaten before going to the stadium to watch a soccer game. This is a ritual that fans perform before going to watch their favorite team play.

#2: Lomito
Available everywhere

The *lomito* has been called the "king of fast food snacks." It sits above the *choripán* both in price and stature. What makes it so regal is that it features the famous beef that Argentina is renowned for.

Street vendor preparing Lomito

At its core, *lomito* is a sirloin steak sandwich that has been flash grilled *a la pancha*. This slab of *lomo* steak is topped with tomatoes, lettuce, onion, *chimichurri*, mayonnaise, fried egg, ham and melted cheese. Quite a mouthful, this is simply one of the most delicious sandwiches you will have on your trip.

Milanesa Sandwich

#3: Milanesa Sandwich
Available everywhere, available vegetarian

If you love the *milanesa*, you will absolutely enjoy the *milanesa* sandwich which is also called *milanga*. You will find it at corner fast food joints or in fast food restaurants.

The *milanesa* sandwich is made with white bread, baguette style. The slice of *milanesa* is put between bread with some lettuce, tomatoes, and mayonnaise. If you include an egg, it is called a *completo*.

If you are vegetarian or are looking for a meat-free option, you can get the *milanesa* sandwich made with soy *milanesa* instead.

#4: Pancho
Available everywhere

The Argentine street food scene would not be complete without a hotdog. The *pancho* is a simple hotdog that is not much more than a frankfurter in a bun. You can sprinkle very thinly cut fried potatoes called *lluvia de papa* (potato rain) to give this sandwich a little more depth.

The more toppings you add on your hotdog transforms it to a "*super pancho*." There are several yummy sauces that go along with this dog. The most popular is the *salsa golf* which is basically a mixture of mayonnaise, mustard and ketchup.

The *pancho* is a favorite as a late night drunken fare. Feel free to try it sober.

#5: Sandwich de Miga and Tostadas
Available everywhere

Extremely popular, you will find these sandwiches at almost every bakery in the country.

These sandwiches look like tea sandwiches but are much bigger. They are made with thinly sliced bread with the crust and edges cut off.

Tostadas

The name *sandwich de miga* translates to "crustless sandwiches." According to the **Academia Argentina de Gastronomia**, these sandwiches are said to have originated in Turin, Italy and were brought to Argentina by Italian immigrants.

The bread used is unique and unlike any bread you would find in the U.S. It is extremely white, very thin and delicately light. The fillings used vary and include ham and cheese, eggs, mayonnaise, olives, tuna and more. You can also find uncommon toppings like prosciutto, pastrami or anchovies. One of the most unique and surprising things about the sandwiches is that you can get them with two slices of bread or three slices.

If you are looking for hot sandwich, duck into a cafe and order the *tostadas*. *Tostadas* are the toasted version of *sandwich de miga*. Try the *tostadas con jamón y queso*. This comes with four delicious toasted ham and cheese sandwiches.

Bondiola

#6: Bondiola
Available everywhere

One sandwich that rivals the **choripán** in popularity is the *bondiola* sandwich, also referred to as *bondipan*. It is a slice of roasted pork shoulder, served on bread, accompanied with lemon juice.

You can enjoy this sandwich in two ways. Order it with toppings like cheese, thinly cut french fries or a fried egg. Or, you can have it plain and dress it up with toppings like *salsa criolla* (a mixture of chopped tomatoes and onions) or **chimichurri** sauce. All this meaty goodness is jammed inside a baguette style loaf and devoured.

You will find it difficult to choose between the *choripán* and *bondiola*; plan on giving yourself enough days to try them both.

#7: Tortilla
Available everywhere, available vegetarian

You will find *tortillas* only in the northwest region of Argentina. *Tortillas* are flatbreads made of wheat flour baked on a **parrilla** (barbeque).

Tortilla on the grill

You can get them plain, but the best are the ones filled with *jamon y queso* (ham and cheese). If you are looking for vegetarian options, you can get tortillas filled with tomatoes, onions, and eggplants.

Served hot off the grill, these *tortillas* will melt in your mouth. Be sure to eat them quickly when they are still hot.

You will find street vendors selling *tortillas* near bus stations, street corners markets or any touristy locations. The vendors usually sell the *tortillas* for *media tarde* (afternoon snack time). Don't miss your window of time as they sell out pretty fast.

Vendor selling pizza by the slice

#8: Pizza by the Slice
Available everywhere, available vegetarian

Pizza is also sold by the slice as an Argentine street food. Called *pizza al paso* or *pizza al corte*, you will find it in fast food joints selling *empanadas* and pizzas. *Pizza al paso* at traditional restaurants is designed to be eaten standing up at the bar with a glass of wine. (And if you skipped how great the Argentine-styled pizza is, go back and learn about it as an authentic speciality.)

#9: Empanadas
Available everywhere, available vegetarian

Empanadas are much loved for their taste and lauded for their portability. You will fall in love with these small and easy to eat Argentine street foods.

Empanadas

One of the best things about the *empanadas* is that they are delicious and made with simple ingredients. You can choose non-vegetarian *empanadas* filled with beef, chicken, ham or more. You will also find vegetarian options stuffed with cheese, spinach and a variety of other mixed vegetables.

Garrapiñadas vendor

#10. Garrapiñadas

For a sweet treat, find a *garrapiñada* stand. Pick up a hot packet fresh from the vendor, and inside you will find caramelized peanuts (*garrapiñada de mani*) or almonds (*garrapiñada de almendras*) that are crunchy and sweet from the sugar coating and fragrant with vanilla essence.

You will find street vendors selling *garrapiñadas* at street fairs or markets during the cooler fall and winter months. They are sold hot right off the pan as a nice snack to have on the go if you have a sweet tooth like most Argentines!

Desserts (Postres)

- **#1:** Dulce de Leche
- **#2:** Alfajores
- **#3:** Facturas & Medialunas
- **#4:** Helados
- **#5:** Chocolates
- **#6:** Chocotorta
- **#7:** Flan
- **#8:** Vigilante
- **#9:** Rogel
- **#10:** Dulce de Membrillo
- **#11:** Dulce de Cajote & Quesillo con Cajote

#1: Dulce de Leche
Available everywhere

Artisanal dulce de leche by Tota

You cannot miss *dulce de leche* when you come to Argentina. It is everywhere and used in all types of desserts and sweets. *Dulce de leche* translates to "sweetness of milk". It is made from sweetened milk that is heated and becomes caramelized to create this nice sweet caramel milk paste. It is eaten practically at every meal, including breakfast where it is spread on bread or toast.

You will easily find dulce de leche at all supermarkets. While all Argentines would agree that *dulce de leche* is legendary, each one has their own preferred brand. One of the reasons why Argentine *dulce de leche* is so good and famous is because of the high quality of the dairy cows. The richer milk makes for a superior quality of *dulce de leche*.

For an authentic experience try a homemade or artisanal version. Skip the industrial supermarket versions and choose artisanal brands. Or better yet, order homemade *dulce de leche* from María Ana Gianni at **Tota Alimentos y Bebidas** (see **Destinations, Buenos Aires**).

Fun Facts About Dulce de Leche

- Since 2006, the average Argentine has eaten about three kilos (roughly six pounds) of *dulce de leche* per year.
- One of the best things to make with dulce de leche is *Panqueques de Dulce de Leche*. This is a very popular Argentine dessert and it is delicious crepes filled with *dulce de leche*.
- *Dulce de Leche* is Argentina's most popular ice cream flavor.

#2: Alfajores
Available everywhere

Alfajores are some of the most prevalent sweet specialities in Argentina. They are two delicious cookies (made with cornstarch), joined together with a thick layer of dulce de leche.

Alfajores

You will find many versions and variations of alfajores in South and Central America including Argentina, Uruguay, Chile, Peru, Paraguay and more. Some are cakey, others are buttery.

The best *alfajores* in Argentina (our humble opinion) are *alfajores de maizena* which are made with corn starch, rolled in coconut shavings, and sprinkled with powdered sugar.

Some of the different variations you will find in Argentina are alfajores coated with dark or white chocolate, or *alfajores* covered with just coconut or sugar powder.

In Argentina *alfajores* are eaten all the time. They are eaten for breakfast, as a dessert at lunch or dinner, or as a snack to accompany tea, coffee or mate throughout the day.

You will find *alfajores* sold at *panaderías* (bakeries) as well as cafés and restaurants. You will also find them at speciality stores like Havana, which has some of the best in Argentina.

Although they are rich and sweet, they are not overwhelmingly sugary. Once you've eaten one, be warned, it will become very easy to eat several every day.

Fun Facts About Alfajores

- Cities around Argentina add their own unique ingredients to *alfajores*. For example in Córdoba, the traditional filling is fruit jam instead of dulce de leche (normally, apple, pear or quince jam)
- Argentines eat the most *alfajores* in the world
- Havanna *alfajores* are the most popular brand in Argentina. They are the pride and joy of Argentines, with most locals calling them the best *alfajores* in the world.

Recipe

Learn to make authentic alfajores with this delicious recipe shared with us by the farm manager's wife, Maria Janariz, when we attended the *asado* at the *estancia* La Manga in Tandil. It's a traditional recipe courtesy of Chef Mario Villalba. Original measurements were provided in grams, but we have converted them to ounce and cup measurements.

MAIZENA ALFAJORES WITH DULCE DE LECHE AND COCONUT FLAKES

Makes between 20-30 alfajores, enough for six people

- 10.5 oz butter (150 grams)
- 1 ½ cups powdered sugar (100 grams)
- 4 eggs
- 1 tsp vanilla extract
- 1 cup flour (100 grams)
- 1 ½ cups cornstarch (250 grams)
- Dulce de leche, as needed
- Grated coconut, as needed

Beat the butter and sugar together with an electric mixer. Add the eggs and continue beating, then add the vanilla, flour and cornstarch. Combine thoroughly.

Cover a work surface with parchment paper, put the dough on it, and cover the dough with another sheet of parchment paper to prevent sticking. Use a rolling pin to stretch the dough to 8 mm (⅓ in) thick. Refrigerate for an hour. Preheat oven to 190°C (370°F). Remove the dough from the refrigerator, and using a round cookie cutter, make cookies of 4-5 cm (1.5-2 in) in diameter. Place them on a baking pan lined with parchment paper and bake 15-20 min, until brown around the edges. Remove and let them cool. Carefully spread dulce de leche on one cookie and cover with a second cookie. Roll in grated coconut.

Visit **authenticfoodquest.com/argentinabook** for the recipe in Spanish.

#3: Facturas & Medialunas

Available everywhere

Breakfast in Argentina is a simple affair. It often involves coffee, orange juice and one of two delicious pastries: the often cream-filled *fracturas* and the crescent-shaped *medialunas*. They are also a popular snack to enjoy throughout the day.

Facturas

Facturas is the name given to little pastries that are found at the many *panaderías* around the country. These little pastries are often sold individually or by the dozen.

You will find these little pastries filled with *dulce de leche*, *crema pastelera* (custard) or *dulce de membrillo*. You can also find them plain and without any filling.

It's worth buying them by the dozen to sample the different types. (It is also more economical making it a good excuse to buy more.)

Facturas and Medialunas at bakery, Buenos Aires

Medialunas

Medialuna means "half moon," and these pastries have a shape similar to French croissants. Compared to French croissants, they are a tad sweeter and a little more doughy.

There are two main types of *medialunas*: *manteca* made with butter, or *grasa* made with vegetable fat. The *manteca* kinds are sweeter and fattier, while the *grasa* are a little more savory.

Medialunas are also found at panaderías and often sold by the dozen. Like *facturas*, they are eaten with coffee at breakfast or at *merienda* (afternoon tea). At *merienda* time, you can also get *medialunas* stuffed with ham and cheese instead. They are usually served with *café con leche* (coffee with milk). If you are in Buenos Aires, some of the best *medialunas* and *fracturas* can be found at **Ninina** in the Palermo neighborhood (see Destinations, Buenos Aires).

Heladería Cadore

#4: Helados
Available everywhere

In every city in Argentina, you will see *heladerías* lining the streets, and you'll also notice motorcycles with little climate controlled boxes zipping around: ice cream parlors delivering *helados* to their customers through most of the day and night.

This is because the ice-cream in Argentina is not "good"—it is outstanding, and some of the best you will find in the world. Brought to Argentina by Italian immigrants, this ice cream is much closer in style to Italian gelato than the typical ice cream you would find in the U.S.

Prepared with whole milk, it is very creamy and thick. Across the board, *heladerías* (ice cream parlors) use high quality and natural ingredients and very little artificial flavors or preservatives.

The oldest artisanal store, **Heladería Cadore** (see Destinations, Buenos Aires) was opened in 1957, and so prized is its heritage that it is distinguished as a landmark by the Cultural Administration of Buenos Aires.

But the best *heladería* (arguably) is **Helados Jauja** (see Destinations, Buenos Aires and Patagonia). This family owned artisanal store makes fresh *helado* daily and uses all natural products sourced from the Patagonia region.

For an authentic *helados* experience, visit their stores and try flavors made with berries from the Patagonian forest and fresh sheep's milk from a family farm in El Calafate. They even have thirteen different chocolate flavors!

The most popular ice cream chains that you will find are **Freddo, Persicco** or **Un Altra Volta** (see Destinations, Buenos Aires). Apparently, the three stores were once owned by two brothers and one business associate. When one of the partners passed away, the stores were divided up with one store getting the signature recipes, the other getting the cash and the final one the unique flavors. Regardless of whichever one you choose to visit, they all stem from the same root and you will not go wrong with the *helados* from any of them.

Helados: Ordering & Delivery

One of thing that you will find surprising is that you can order ice-cream by the kilo at the various *heladerias*. You will also be able to order your typical cones and cups, but having the 1 or 2 kilo tubs is quite a treat, especially in the sweltering summer heat.

Most *heladerias* in Argentina deliver ice-cream (using the motorcycle carriers mentioned above). Although you will never be too far from a *heladeria*, it is worth trying the delivery service at least once on your trip.

Flavors:
Dulce de Leche

To eat ice cream like an Argentine, order ***dulce de leche***, the most popular flavor. *Dulce de leche* does not just come in one velvety textured flavor. You will be amazed at the different *dulce de leche* variations available. You can get *dulce de leche* with nuts, double *dulce de leche*, *dulce de leche* with chocolate and much more.

Specialty Flavors

In different regions across the across the country, artisanal *heladerías* create signature flavors to match the local and regional specialities. For example, in

Mendoza, you will find *helados* flavored with Malbec wine. In Cafayate, you can try it flavored with Torrontés wine. You will also find **yerba mate** and **fernet**.

Traditional Rama Chocolates

#5: Chocolates
Patagonia and the Lake Region

Bariloche in the southwest part of Argentina is commonly referred to as "Little Switzerland." This reference is in part due to the European immigrants, weather, architecture and chocolates.

The most famous street in Bariloche is Mitre Avenue, or what Argentines call "The Avenue of Chocolate Dreams." This street is lined with several dozen chocolate stores and chocolate will tempt you in every direction. With so many stores to choose from, your dilemma will be how you will get through it all.

While sampling the different types of chocolates, be sure to leave plenty of room for the local chocolate speciality. Bariloche is famous for the traditional *rama* chocolates which are also referred to as "cigars" or chocolate "flakes".

The chocolates are rich, creamy and delicious and made with with real cocoa butter. Be sure to taste Bariloche on your travels. See section 3 for recommendations of chocolate stores to visit.

Museo Del Chocolate

To complement your visits to the chocolate stores, learn even more about the history of chocolate in Central and South America at the **Museo del Chocolate** (see Destinations, Patagonia/Bariloche).

Now called the Havanna Museo del Chocolate after a popular brand of chocolates and *alfajores*, it was formerly the Fenoglio Museo del Chocolate, named in tribute to Aldo Feneglio and his wife who were key founders of chocolate in Bariloche.

Fun Facts About Chocolates in Bariloche

- Stores freely give out samples of their chocolates; make sure to taste before you buy.

- The Guinness Book's World's Largest Easter Egg was made in Bariloche in 2012. It is reported to have been over 8.5 m (27 ft) high and 5 m (16 ft) wide, made with over 4,000 kg (8,800 lbs) of chocolate.

- Try a "Submarino." This is a classic drink with a chocolate bar immersed in hot milk.

#6: Chocotorta
Available everywhere

Roughly translated to "chocolate cake," this birthday party staple only has three ingredients: **dulce de leche**, *queso crema* (Argentina cream cheese) and *chocolinas* (chocolate cookies).

This easy dessert is made by soaking the chocolate cookies in milk and layering them in the bottom of a pan, followed by a layer of *dulce de leche* mixed with the *queso crema* or a cream cheese equivalent. Continue layering alternating between cookies and dulce de leche mixed with cream cheese. Once the top of the dish is reached, place the cake in the freezer for at least one hour.

There are variations to this classic *chocotorta*. Instead of milk, the *chocolinas* can be soaked in coffee or Kahlúa (coffee flavored liqueur) for a more adult version.

You will not typically find this cake on the dessert menus are restaurants, though it is something Argentines consume regularly at home or in private settings. Like an **asado** or **mate**, find a way to get invited to a get together with locals and experience this delight.

#7: Flan
Available everywhere

Flan with dulce de leche

On your visit to Argentina, you will see *flan* on almost every menu. Behind *alfajores*, *flan* ranks in the top category for most common and popular Argentine desserts.

Bearing similarities to French crème caramel, *flan* is a custard made with a sweetened mix of eggs, milk, and sugar, flavored with vanilla extract. A thin layer of soft caramels tops the flan. In addition to being popular in Argentina, it is also a favorite dessert in other South American countries as well as Spain.

This is a popular grand finale to any meal at a restaurant or at home, and in Argentina it always comes with huge serving of **dulce de leche**. When your server asks if you want your *flan* with or without *dulce de leche*, eat like the Argentines and never decline it.

Vigilante

#8: Vigilante
Available everywhere

Though you will not find this unique treat on restaurant menus, it is one of Argentina's most emblematic desserts and is very simple to make at home.

Vigilante consists of a simple slice of sweet paste and another of cheese. The sweet paste is placed on top and it can be either *dulce de batata* (sweet potato paste) or **dulce de membrillo** (quince paste), which you will read about later in this section.

The second component is a slice of *queso* or cheese that is similar to a Gouda. This block of cheese is known as *pategrás*. You can also have it with a softer and creamier cheese known as *queso cremoso*.

For the best combination, use the *pategrás* cheese and the *dulce de batata*. You will not find it intensely sweet (and it does not taste like a potato). Be prepared for the unusual and delicious combination of textures and flavors.

#9: Rogel
Available everywhere

This is a very original dessert, beautiful and impressive to look at and a classic "cake" at Argentine weddings and special events.

The main ingredient is the national treasure, **dulce de leche**, layered on paper thin pastry.

Layer upon layer is piled up until you arrive at the last level, which is a decadent layer of whipped Italian meringue.

If you don't find it at cafés, restaurants and bakeries, don't give up on your search. Rogel is not very easy to find, but it is worth hunting down.

Once you bite into this dessert, the layers of pastry and the gooey dulce de leche and meringue, will provide every texture you want from a single dessert.

Be warned however, this cake is designed for those who have a sweet tooth. Do make a point to try this traditional dessert on your trip to Argentina.

#10: Dulce de Membrillo
Available everywhere

This dessert is off the beaten path and is based on the fruit called *membrillo* (or quince in English). This fruit looks like a bumpy pear and though it is not sweet in its raw state, it is transformed when peeled and cooked with a generous amount of sugar. The flesh softens and turns into a gorgeous pink color, and the high levels of pectin allow the quince to firm up, making it ideal for jams and jellies.

While *membrillo* or quince is not popular in the U.S, it thrives in Argentina. Argentina actually ranks among the world's top ten producers of quince.

The most popular culinary use for quince in Argentina is *dulce de membrillo*. It is not too sweet and a popular filling for *facturas*, tarts, and sweet pastries such as *pastelitos*. It is also sold as a paste for *budin* (cake) or **vigilante**.

#11: Dulce de Cajote & Quesillo con Cajote
The Wine Regions and The Andean Northwest

The *cajote* (pronounced ka-chote) is a fibrous fruit that looks similar to a watermelon. It is cooked with sugar and is used to make a type of marmalade for various desserts. The resulting *dulce de cajote* is popular in the provinces of Salta and Jujuy.

Quesillo con cajote

Mix the *dulce de cajote* with the native cheese *quesillo*, and you get the delightful dessert *quesillo con cajote*.

The *quesillo* is a flat cheese made from a combination of cow and goat milk, and in one variation pictured below, the chef added walnuts, calling it *cayote con quesillo y nuez*.

Cayote con Quesillo y Nuez

The combination of sweet from the jam and salt from the cheese makes this dessert quite exquisite, and the crunchiness of the walnuts added here is divine.

Unique Produce

#1: Andean Potatoes (Papas Andinas)
#2: Quinoa
#3: Corn (Maiz)
#4: Goat Cheese (Queso de Cabra)

#1: Andean Potatoes (Papas Andinas)
The Andean Northwest

Tucked against the Andes, northwest Argentina is dry and arid, making it home to diverse produce adapted to the climate. The native potatoes, or *papas andinas*, have been grown by indigenous peoples for centuries. Despite the harsh conditions, they developed farming techniques to grow potatoes, corn, quinoa, and more.

Andean Potatoes Varieties, Tilcara Farmers Market

Farmers markets in the Salta and Jujuy provinces feature andean potatoes or *papas andinas* in a colorful array of green, red, and even black skins.

These native potatoes grow in high altitudes (as high as 3,000 meters or nearly 10,000 feet) making them resistant to diseases. They are also exposed to intense cold temperatures at night and intense heat during the day, concentrating minerals such as calcium and potassium.

Some of the popular varieties you will see are in the region are:

- ***Papas oca:*** These yellow or red varieties taste slightly sweet and will practically melt in your mouth after they are cooked. Delicious.
- ***Papas verdes:*** Small and green, these potatoes have a neutral flavor.
- ***Papas churquenas:*** This most popular variety is small, round and yellow, and used in many regional dishes. Like the *papas ocas*, these are tasty.

VIDEO - COOKING ANDEAN POTATOES

In a short video you can see the beautiful colors of *papas andinas* we got from the Mercado Municipal in Tilcara (Jujuy Province). We enjoyed them with a tomato salad, **queso de cabra**, and *salame de* **llama**… *Riquisimo*!

View the video at **authenticfoodquest.com/argentinabook**.

#2: Quinoa
Andean Northwest

Quinoa Salad in Humahuaca

Quinoa is known as the "Golden Grain of The Andes", and it was the daily diet of Inca civilizations more than 5,000 years ago. Today, quinoa is growing in popularity as a health food or "superfood" that is highly regarded for it's high protein content and delicious nutty flavors.

Quinoa is also gluten-free making it ideal for celiacs, vegetarians and vegans. So important is this grain that in 2013, The United Nations General Assembly declared 2013 as the "International Year of Quinoa", in recognition of ancestral practices of the Andean people, who have managed to preserve quinoa in its natural state as food for present and future generations, through ancestral practices of living in harmony with nature.

Quinoa is actually found in all countries of the Andes region which include Argentina, Bolivia, Chile, Columbia, Ecuador and Peru. On your travels to the northwest region of Argentina, be sure to visit the local farmers markets. You will be surprised to discover different types of varieties and unusual quinoa based products. See Destinations for the list of farmers markets in the area.

Try these unusual quinoa based regional delicacies.

Quinoa Empanadas
The local *empanada* speciality in this region is the the *empanada de quinoa*. Seek it out on your travels and enjoy the delicious crunchy texture and hearty flavors.

Quinoa Salad
The *ensalada de quinoa* is simple and refreshing, made with quinoa, tomatoes, corn, and local Andean cheese.

Quinoa Soup
In the cool evenings, warm up with quinoa soup or *sopa de quinoa*, a hearty soup with mixed vegetables that makes a healthy treat.

Quinoa Alfajores
Given the popularity of *alfajores* in Argentina, it is no surprise that a quinoa version exists. Look for these unique quinoa-based *alfajores,* and keep in

mind that while quinoa may be healthy, these little treats are still filled with *dulce de leche*. The quinoa gives this cookie a nutty regional twist.

#3: Corn (Maiz)
Andean Northwest

Maiz, or corn, is a base ingredient in many folk dishes, but its importance extends far beyond food. *Maiz* plays a role in traditional ceremonies and religious rituals, and builds the collective identity of native Andean people.

Corn Varieties, Tilcara Farmers Market

Today, a lot of varieties are disappearing due to the introduction of GMO varieties that have a better yield. The villages of the *Quebrada de Humahuaca* in the province of Jujuy are making a concerted effort to hold onto their traditions by cultivating the different varieties of *maiz* in their *quintas* (vegetable gardens). These little gardens keep the tradition and the culture of *maiz* alive.

As you make your way through the local farmers markets, take the time to appreciate the many varieties of *maiz*. You will be surprised to see a wide variety of colors on more than ten varieties. The "ear of corn", called *choclo* in the native language of *Quechua*, is the delicious filling used in the **humitas, tamales** and **empanadas** in the region.

#4: Goat Cheese (Queso de Cabra)
Andean Northwest

As you drive through the northwest region of Argentina, you will see many goats grazing the hillsides, which is indication of the widespread availability of the goat cheese. At roadside markets, local older ladies sell *queso de cabra* with rounds of homemade flat bread called *pan casero*.

Goat Cheese / Pan Casero

The goat cheese is delicious and different from the soft kind that you typically find in the U.S., much firmer with a grassy flavor.

For a local experience, you can visit a goat farm in Cafayate, which is also the second wine producing region in the country. At **Cabras de Cafayate** (see **Destinations, Cafayate**), you will get a tour of the goat farm and learn how goat cheese is made. The farm tour ends with a tasting of a variety of goat cheeses.

Beverages

#1: Mate
#2: Malbec
#3: Torrontés
#4: Argentine Beers
#5: Fernet Branca
#6: Argentina Mineral Water

#1: Mate

Available everywhere

The native Guarani Indian people call it the "Drink of the Gods," and are said to have survived periods of drought and famine by drinking *yerba mate*. For the Argentine gauchos, it is known as their "liquid vegetable." *Mate* (pronounced 'MAH-tay') is an infusion of dried leaves of the yerba mate (Ilex paraguariensis) plant, and you will see people walking around holding a little gourd and sipping their *mate* from a metal straw.

Mate

The leaves of the yerba mate tree contain over 24 vitamins and minerals, 15 amino acids, abundant antioxidants and naturally occurring caffeine. Many benefits are touted, including its ability to reduce fatigue, suppress appetite, and protect against colds and the flu.

How To Drink Mate

The drinking of *mate* with friends is an important social ritual in Argentina. There is a particular set of social codes to follow when drinking this shared beverage. One person is the server—usually the person who owns the gourd and also prepares the *mate*—and he or she fills it for each person. Each person drinks the full serving before passing it back to the server. Everybody uses the same gourd and straw, and says "*gracias*" after they have had their fill.

Mate is typically consumed hot, but it can also be consumed as a cold beverage, called *terrere*, which is popular in Paraguay. Traditionally, *mate* is consumed without sugar. However, you may add sugar, honey or even orange or lemon zest for additional flavor.

Where To Try Mate

Despite its popularity, you will not find mate as a menu item at most establishments. It is more of an everyday social drink, enjoyed amongst friends.

That said, you can ask for it off the menu, and you will find some restaurants and cafés willing to allow you to sample this tradition. If you end up enjoying this drink, don't hesitate to purchase a gourd and straw at any of the markets. You will find long aisles in the local grocery stores dedicated to *yerba mate*. In the U.S., you will find yerba mate available at many local and chain grocery stores.

#2: Malbec
Mendoza region

The grape variety originally comes from the Cahors region in the southwest of France. It was introduced into Argentina in 1852 by Michel Pouget, a French agronomist hired by the Argentine government. When phylloxera disease destroyed the French viticulture towards the end of the 19th century, the grape variety was thought to have disappeared. Fortunately, it had taken hold in Argentina.

What makes Malbec so popular is how easy it is to drink and how well it goes with or without food. Malbec pairs well with red meats, grilled meats, hard cheeses and pasta with tomato sauce.

During the economic turbulent period of the early 2000s, the price of wines rose and many Americans sought affordable delicious alternatives. This propelled the growth of Malbec. It was popularized not by sommeliers, but by regular wine drinkers.

Malbec Tasting Experience

Malbec wines have Controlled Denomination of Origin (DOC) in some Argentine regions. This helps to protect the name of the area and forces winemakers to maintain the high quality of the wines.

The most significant characteristic of Malbec is its intense dark color. In the mouth, Malbec is warm, soft and non-aggressive. It has intense fruity flavors and a velvety texture.

Malbec wine expresses itself very differently around the world. For example, a study by the University of California, Davis found that there are distinct flavors and compositional differences between Malbec wines produced in Mendoza and California. Therefore, it is crucial to try this wine directly from the source. See **Destinations** for recommendations on winery tours.

> **Fun Facts About Argentina and Malbec Wines**
> - Argentina has the largest Malbec acreage in the world.
> - Malbec Wine Day in Argentina is celebrated every April 17th.
> - It took Argentina 150 years from the first vines of Malbec to produce a decent wine for export.

#3: Torrontés
Cafayate

Torrontés is the most famous white wine in Argentina, and this grape varietal is produced nowhere else in the world but in Argentina.

Aromatic and light, Torrontés is yellowish in color, with golden and green hues. The wine has sweet and floral aromas that range from white peach and grapefruit to tangerine. Though it smells sweet, this wine has a surprisingly dry style and a refreshing finish.

Torrontés is an ideal wine for a variety of foods. It is light enough to go with fish, chicken or Asian cuisine, yet sturdy enough to handle red meats and Argentine *asados*.

The best Torrontés wines come from the high elevation vineyards of the Cafayate Valley, in Salta Province. The vineyards are the highest vineyards in the world and with scarce rainfall, these conditions allow for an exceptional development of grapevines. The wines of Cafayate have a strong personality and linger in the mouth.

There are three kinds of Torrontés in Argentina: *Torrontés Riojano*, *Torrontés Sanjuanino* and *Torrontés Mendocino*. Of the three varieties, the most popular and delicious is the Torrontés Riojano grape which grows in Salta. The are said to be much simpler in aroma and taste and often made in a sweet style.

> **Fun Facts About Cafayate and Torrontés**
> - Cafayate has over 340 sunny days per year and is referred to as *"the land where the sun lives."*
> - Be sure to taste Torrontés flavored ice-cream at **Dessio** and **Helado Miranda**, the artisanal *heladerías* in the main plaza in Cafayate. Get the addresses in the Cafayate section of **Destinations**.

#4: Argentine Beers
Patagonia and the Lake Region

While Argentina is known for its Malbec wine, beer is also a very popular drink to share with friends over an ***asado***.

Beers from Patagonia

The national beer, is a brand called Quilmes, founded in 1888 by German immigrant, Otto Bemberg. It took its name from a small city in the province of Buenos Aires known for having high quality water. The beer grew to become the most popular beer in Buenos Aires and then in all of Argentina. Today, it is like a national symbol and represents 67% of the beer market in Argentina.

But despite national beer roots in Buenos Aires, Bariloche in Patagonia is the main craft beer city. There are fifteen microbreweries producing and selling beer at local pubs. Home-brewed beer (*cerveza artesanal*) is growing particularly around Bariloche and El Bolsón (situated 70 km / 43 mi south of Bariloche). To celebrate the beer heritage in the area, Bariloche hosts the National Outdoor Beer Festival in December. Check the Bariloche section in **Destinations** for details.

Draft beers in Argentina are called *chopp*. They are available in three main types: *cerveza rubia* (red ale), *colorada* (pale lager) and *negra* (stout). You will find a surprising array of flavors and beer is served at dedicated bars called *cervecerías*.

Beer in Argentina often comes in large one-liter bottles. These bottles are meant for sharing. If you want a small single serve bottle, ask for a *porrón*.

The chart below highlights prominent beers you'll likely see at bars and *cervecerías* across Argentina.

BRAND	STYLE	REGION	NOTES
Quilmes	Lager	National	The national beer, this is a light lager without much taste.
Imperial	Weissbier Red Lager Scotch Ale Stout	Buenos Aires	Produced by the second largest beer producer in Argentina called CCU Argentina. A step above Quilmes.
Norte	Lager	Salta & Jujuy	Produced by Quilmes. Taste identical to Quilmes.
Salta	Lager Stout	Salta	Great to drink with empanadas salteñas.
Schneider	Pale Ale Red Ale Stout	National	Originally produced in Santa Fe, it is now CCU Argentina (the second producer of beer in Argentina) most popular brand.
Antares	Various craft brews	National	The leader of craft beers in Argentina. Originated in 1994 in Mar del Plata, the brewery now has 32 locations.
Cape Horn	Pale Ale Red Ale Stout	Patagonia & the Lakes	Named after the southernmost headland above the Drake Passage.
Beagle	Wheat Pale Ale Stout	Patagonia & the Lakes	Named after the Beagle Channel that separates Argentina from Chile, and connects the Atlantic and Pacific. Beagle and Cape Horn are both produced locally by Cerveceria Beagle in Ushuaia.
Patagonia	Wheat Amber Stout	Patagonia & the Lakes	Produced by Quilmes, Patagonia is their craft beer.
Berlina	Various craft brews	Patagonia & the Lakes	One of the most successful microbreweries of Bariloche. You can visit their microbrewery in Colonia Suiza (see Destinations).

#5: Fernet Branca
Available everywhere

Dark and syrupy with a slightly medicinal black licorice taste, Fernet Branca (or just "fernet" to locals) originated in Italy, and made its way to Argentina with European immigrants in the late 19th century. It is a popular liqueur in Argentina consumed by grandparents and college students alike, and it is a regular fixture at ***asados***.

In Argentina, fernet is traditionally mixed with Coca-Cola in an ice filled glass that is sometimes referred to as *fernicola* or *fernet con cola*.

Get a feel for fernet on your travels to Argentina and be sure to experience this national cocktail.

Fernet

Fun Facts About Fernet

- Fernet is so popular in Argentina that the country consumes more than 75% of all Fernet produced globally.
- Fernet is so important in Argentina that in 2014 it was added to a price-freeze program to protect it from skyrocketing inflation.
- The city of Cordoba in Central Argentina has a strong Italian heritage, and consumes more fernet than all of Italy.

#6: Argentina Mineral Water
Available everywhere

Bottled water is widely available throughout Argentina. As you are traveling through the country and enjoying the local food delicacies, be sure to make the bottled waters from Argentina a companion to your meal.

The two most popular brands of mineral water are Villavicencio and Eco de los Andes, which are both bottled in the country.

Villavicencio

Villavicencio, is the most widely sold brand, comes from a protected natural reserve at the foothills of the Andes mountains just outside of Mendoza. On the protected natural reserve is The **Gran Hotel de Villavicencio** (see **Destinations, Mendoza**). This was a popular resort in the 1940s where wealthy families would bathe in the mountain waters and natural hot springs.

The hotel today is a national historic monument and it is worth a trip to see where the delicious water you are drinking comes from.

Eco de los Andes

Eco de los Andes is another important brand of mineral water in Argentina. This water comes from the natural springs in the Andes in Mendoza. Widely available, you can get it as still or sparkling mineral water.

Gota

Gota is a super premium natural mineral water brand from Argentina. The water is sourced from the region of the Iguazú Falls. You will see their artistic water bottles at upscale stores and restaurants. This water is notably clean and smooth tasting.

Villavicencio / Eco les Andes / Gotta Water

3. DESTINATIONS
Where To Eat Across Argentina

BUENOS AIRES & THE PAMPAS
  Buenos Aires - The Multicultural Capital
  Tandil - Land of the Gauchos

THE WINE REGIONS
  Mendoza - Malbec's Roots
  Cafayate - The Origin of Torrontés

THE ANDEAN NORTHWEST REGION
  Salta - "Salta the Beautiful"
  Cachi - Enchanted Valley
  Jujuy Province - An UNESCO Heritage Gorge

PATAGONIA & THE LAKE REGION
  Bariloche - "Little Switzerland" in Patagonia
  Colonia Suiza - The Swiss Colony
  El Calafate - A Glacial Hub
  Ushuaia - The Town at the End of the World

Buenos Aires & the Pampas

BUENOS AIRES

Known for its European-style architecture and rich cultural life, Buenos Aires defines itself as a multicultural city, with great influence from European immigrants primarily from Italy, Spain and Germany. It is considered as one of the most diverse cities in Latin America.

Buenos Aires and The Pampas, based on B1mbo work

Buenos Aires is the capital and largest city of Argentina, with a population of about 2.9 million people. It is located on the western shore of the estuary of the Río de la Plata, on the continent's southeastern coast. It is a top tourist destination and the most visited city in South America.

The cuisine in Buenos Aires cuisine is largely influenced by its European heritage and has been developed with a distinctively Argentine nuance.

FARMERS MARKETS

Organic Farmers Markets

Feria Organica San Telmo Verde

This small covered market showcases twenty stands with organic products. Here you will find fresh bread, *tartas* (quiches), *budin* (sweet cakes), chocolate, cheese, dry cured sausages, grains, dried fruits, and organic drinks and juices.

Address: Peru 677, San Telmo, Buenos Aires
Hours: Tues & Fri from 10am to 5pm
Find them on Facebook: Facebook.com/SanTelmo.Verde

Mercado Solidario Bonpland

This covered market in Palermo has fantastic organic cheeses, pastas, olive oil and vegetables. Although it is open most of the day, it is more lively around lunchtime or after 5pm.

Address: Bonpland 1660, Palermo, Buenos Aires
Hours: Tues, Wed, Fri & Sat 10am to 10pm
Find them on Facebook: Facebook.com/MercadoSolidario.Bonpland

Sabe la Tierra

Held in a working train station (*San Fernando del Tren de la Costa*), this small open-air market straddles the railway tracks. On one side are mostly prepared organic foods, and you can sample organic mediterranean hummus, cheese, fresh juices, lentil soups, artisanal beers and much more. On the other side of the tracks is a small selection of fresh fruits and vegetables. The atmosphere is very convivial, with music playing and tables set up to enjoy the local dishes. This market takes place at several locations in and around Buenos Aires, but the San Fernando market is by far the coolest and most unusual.

Address: Juan N. Madero y Rosario, San Fernando, Buenos Aires
Hours: Sat from 10am to 5pm
Locations in Buenos Aires, Vincente Lopez, & Mazchwitz. Check the website at SabeLaTierra.com for hours & directions.

El Galpon

This market is one of the most popular organic markets in Buenos Aires. It is located on the west side of the city in a warehouse-like building with several producers selling their products. Their **website** provides some insights on what you will find: everything from cheeses to vegetables producers.

Address: Avenida Federico Lacroze 4171, Chacarita, Buenos Aires
Hours: Wed & Sat from 9am to 6pm
ElGalpon.org.ar

Mercado Natural Punto Verde

At this market you will find a variety of organic and healthy products as well as artisanal items. There are more than thirty local producers selling a variety of products.

Address: Avenida Dorrego 1429, Chacarita, Buenos Aires
Hours: Wed, Fri & Sat from 10am to 7pm
MercadoPuntoVerde.com.ar

Mobile Farmers Markets
Buenos Aires Market

The most popular (and trendy) mobile market is the Buenos Aires Market. This market takes place two times a month at different locations in the city. One of the recurring locations is the Hipodromo de Palermo in Buenos Aires. Come for the experience: you can spend the day here, eating prepared meals from different vendors and enjoying a variety of sweets. Various locations throughout the city; check the website for updates on location and hours.
BuenosAiresMarket.com

Permanent Farmers Markets
Mercado de San Telmo

Located in the historic barrio of San Telmo, this is one of the oldest markets in Buenos Aires. Built in 1897, it was dedicated to serve as a large centralized fruit and vegetable market for immigrants. Today, it is a mix of antique, food and coffee stands along with fruits and vegetables. The fruit and vegetable stands are open all day long, but butchers tend to open only in the morning or after 5pm. It is mostly busy and lively on the weekends, with Saturday being the best day to visit; it might not get as crowded as Sundays.
Address: Defensa y Carlos Calvo, San Telmo, Buenos Aires
Hours: Everyday from 8am to 9pm with most vendors closed during siesta (1pm to 4-5pm)
Turismo.BuenosAires.gob.ar/es/atractivo/Mercado-de-San-Telmo

Mercado del Progreso

Butchers fill this lively market in the Caballito Barrio of Buenos Aires. Among the vibrant, energetic and very animated vendors, you will see several stands with people preparing the famous *milanesa*. This is one of the rare markets with a fish stand, a notable treat since fish is not a staple of the Argentine diet despite proximity to the Atlantic. If you have a craving for fish (or lively atmosphere), this is the place to go.
Address: Av Rivadavia 5430, Caballito, Buenos Aires
Hours: Mon-Sat from 7:30am to 1pm & 5pm to 8:30pm
MercadoDelProgreso.com

FOOD STORES
The Big Stores
Coto

Coto is a popular supermarket chain and a great option for all your shopping needs. It is a modern well-lit store similar to the types of stores you would find in the U.S. You will find a great selection of local specialities and fresh fruit and vegetables.
Coto.com.ar

Disco

Disco is another solid option in the city for your shopping needs. Though not as fancy as Coto, it is still a good option.
Disco.com/ar

Carrefour

This French company has many locations in Buenos Aires. You will also find many of their smaller stores, called **Carrefour Express**. These stores provide some staples but have a limited selection. In general at Carrefour, the aisles are filled with mostly processed foods and not a wide selection of fresh produce; however, it is an option when you are missing a few basic items. Carrefour.com/ar

Chino

Finally, you will also find a breed of *supermercado* referred to as *chino* as they are typically run by Chinese immigrants. They are smaller supermarkets with a limited offerings. Open late into the night, these stores can be convenient when you need just a few basic items at odd hours. Be aware that they may not take credit cards. You will find those *supermercados* in all the neighborhoods of Buenos Aires.

Local Specialty Stores

Panaderías (Bakeries)

There are a huge selection of bakeries in Buenos Aires. Your best bet is to try your neighborhood bakery and let yourself be tempted. If you find yourself craving more baked delicacies beyond our selections below, consult this great list of the best bakeries in Buenos Aires: TheRealArgentina.com/en/The-Best-Confiterias-and-Panaderias-in-Buenos-Aires/

Ninina

This bakery located in Palermo offers creative homemade pastries such as **medialunas** and **alfajores** as well as bread, pies and more.

Address: Gorriti 4738, Buenos Aires, Argentina
Hours: Mon-Fri, 8am to 12am; Sat-Sun, 9am to 12am
Call: +54 114-832-0070   Ninina.com

La Nueva Independencia

This bakery is located in San Telmo with a nice selection of homemade pastries and fresh bread. Check locally for store hours.

Address: Avenida Independencia 467, Buenos Aires, Argentina
Call: +54 114-300-7934

Verdulerías (Fruit and Vegetable Grocers)

Verdulería la Martina

This is a large verdulería with an impressive selection of fruit and vegetables coming from different regions across Argentina.

Address: Avenida Belgrano 1820, Montserrat, Buenos Aires
Hours: Mon-Sat, 8am to 9pm; Sun 9am to 2pm
Call: +54 114-381-6472

Carnicerías (Butchers)

Carnicería Arribas

You can find this long-standing butcher with quality meats in the **Mercado de San Telmo**.

Address: Defensa y Carlos Calvo, Puesto #54, San Telmo, Buenos Aires
Hours: Mon-Sat, 8am to 1pm & 5pm to 8pm
Turismo.BuenosAires.gob.ar/es/Atractivo/Mercado-de-San-Telmo

Carnicería Nucho, "El Rey de la Molleja"

This large carniceria in the **Mercado del Progreso** is always busy with locals buying their daily meat. Nucho is known to have the best *molleja* (sweetbread) in Buenos Aires, which is what makes them "El Rey," the King!

Address: Avenida Rivadavia 5430, Caballito, Buenos Aires
Hours: Mon-Sat from 8am to 1pm & 5pm to 8:30pm
Find them on Facebook: Facebook.com/NuchoCarnicerias

Dietéticas

Dietética Gaia

This store, located next to the San Telmo organic market, offers a nice selection of organic products as well as good organic bread.

Address: Av. Pres. Manuel Quintana 596, Recoleta Buenos Aires
Hours: Mon-Fri, 9am to 8pm; Sat from 10am to 3pm; Closed on Sun
Find them on Facebook: Facebook.com/Gaia.Dietetica

Cheese and cured meat stores

Estancia San Francisco

The variety of cheeses and smoked hams at this chain of Buenos Aires stores is quite amazing!

Address: Avenida Entre Ríos 700, Montserrat, Buenos Aires
Hours: Mon-Sat, 9am to 9pm
ESanFrancisco.com.ar

Pasta Stores

You will find incredible pasta stores all around Buenos Aires that sell fresh pasta, or *pastas artesanales*. These are "real food museums" where you can see how they make the pasta and the *raviol* with antique machines. Going to these stores is a real experience. Visit the pasta stores in your neighborhood; look for long lines and clean stores.

L'Artisan Taller de Pastas

One of the best pasta stores in Buenos Aires, they have a nice selection of fresh pasta made in Argentina. They make *raviol*, but also *sorrentino*, fettucine and *ñoquis*.
Address: Rodríguez Peña 1771, Recoleta,
Buenos Aires
Second location at Arcos 3182, Nuñez, Buenos Aires
Hours: Mon 12pm to 9pm; Tues-Sat, 10pm to 9pm; Sun 10am to 3pm
LartisanTaller.com

Heladerías (Ice Cream Stores)

Nonna Bianca

Try flavors across the region, from the classic sweet **dulce de leche** to the bitter and complex **mate**.

Address: Estados Unidos 425, San Telmo, Buenos Aires
Hours: Daily, 9am to 2am
Find them on Facebook: Facebook.com/pages/Nonna-Bianca/113443168738300

Jauja

Jauja is a famous *heladería* from Patagonia. If your travels do not take you to the Patagonia region, make sure to stop at their store in Buenos Aires. The chocolate

ice creams are scrumptious.
Address: Avenida Cerviño 3901, Palermo, Buenos Aires
Second location at Federico Lacroze 2239, Buenos Aires
Hours: Mon-Fri, 8:30am to 1am; Sat 10:30am to 2am; Sun 11am to 1am
See more at Jauja.com.ar

Heladería Cadore

This is the oldest ice cream store, established in Buenos Aires since 1957 and now a national landmark. It is a very popular store with dozens of flavors to choose from. Make a point to sample the delicious ice cream flavors here.
Address: Avenida Corrientes 1695, Tribunales, Buenos Aires
Hours: Daily from 11:30am to 2am
HeladeriaCadore.com.ar

There are other popular ice-cream chains that you will find across the city:

Freddo: Freddo.com.ar

Persicco: Persicco.com

Un Altra Volta: UnAltraVolta.com.ar

All offer very good ice-cream as well. Go for the local flavors like **dulce de leche, tramontana** (vanilla with *dulce de leche*), and **mate**. Check the websites for locations in your neighborhood and hours.

Seafood Stores

There are not many stand alone seafood stores in the city. You will find seafood mostly sold frozen in supermarkets. For unique and dedicated stores, visit the options listed below.

Cucina di Mare

This seafood store is located in the **Mercado del Progreso**, and you must not miss their homemade paella on Friday nights and Saturday lunches. They sell fresh seafood and prepared meals.
Address: Avenida del Barco Centenera 141, Local 55, Caballito, Buenos Aires
Hours: Tues-Fri, 8am to 1pm & 5pm to 8:30pm; Sat 8am to 2pm
Visit CucinaDiMare.com or email info@cucinadimarelamarina.com.ar

Colucci

Colucci is located in the *barrio centro* of the city. They have a nice presentation of fresh fish and seafood.
Address: Montevideo 270, Centro, Buenos Aires
Hours: Mon-Fri, 11:30am to 3:30pm & 5pm to 8pm. Sat 11:30am to 1:30pm
ColucciPescados.com.ar

Sweet & Savory Deliveries

Tota Alimentos y Bebidas

Nothing beats homemade **dulce de leche**, and you can order it from the fabulous kitchen of Tota Alimentos y Bebidas. The founder, María Ana Gianni, runs this small business making artisanal food (*alimentos*) and drinks (*bebidas*). If you want to be blown away by homemade Argentine delicacies, order directly from her and get your order delivered (Buenos Aires only). The best way to contact her is via her Facebook page, **Facebook.com/TotaAAyBB** where she has gorgeous photos of what she's making. You can also contact her through her email address: **tota.aaybb@gmail.com**

RESTAURANTS

There are endless restaurant options in Buenos Aires, ranging from budget eateries all the way to high-end sophisticated restaurants. The restaurants listed below are some of the best options for authentic and traditional experiences that we tried or were recommended to us by locals.

Parrilla

El Desnivel

The scents of grilling meat greet you at this rustic and popular *parrilla* in San Telmo neighborhood. Every cut you can imagine is grilled on the *parrilla* at the entrance of the restaurant, making you salivate while waiting for your order. The great quality of beef and casual atmosphere attracts locals and travelers alike for the quality meats and atmosphere.

Address: Defensa 855, San Telmo, Buenos Aires
Hours: 12pm to 4pm & 8pm to 1am
Call: +54 114-300-9081
WelcomeSanTelmo.com/san-telmo-guide/rxhjtfw9zq/El-Desnivel
Price Range: $

Gran Parrilla del Plata

Converted from an old butcher shop, this is classic *parrilla* is said to be one of the best in historic San Telmo. It has a simple laid back atmosphere and generous portions of tasty grilled meat. President Obama and Michelle Obama ate at this restaurant on their visit to Argentina in March 2016. You will want to make reservations in advance to experience this *parrilla*.

Address: Chile 594, San Telmo, Buenos Aires
Hours: Mon 8pm to 1am; Tues-Sun 12pm to 4pm & 8pm to 1am
Call: +5411-4300-8858
ParrillaDelPlata.com/home-eng.htm
Price Range: $$$

Las Cabras

This popular restaurant in trendy Palermo offers large cuts of meat to share at very affordable prices. It has a large *parrilla* inside the restaurant and a quaint rustic decor. There is also a patio for dining out. Try their *empanadas* made *al horno*. This is a nice alternative to the rather fancy and pricey *parrillas* around Palermo. Reservations recommended.

Address: Fitz Roy 1795, Palermo, Buenos Aires
Hours: Mon to Sun 12pm to 1am
Call: +54-115-197-5301/5303
TimeOut.com/Buenos-Aires/restaurants-cafes/venue/1%3A26943/Las-Cabras
Price Range: $

El Pobre Luis

This is a recommended *parrilla* in the Chinese neighborhood (Barrio Chino) which stands out in the midst of many of the Chinese and Thai restaurants. Highly recommended by locals as one of the best of Buenos Aires, go early and wait in line. Be patient to get a table or make reservations ahead of time.

Address: Arribeños 2393, Belgrano, Buenos Aires
Hours: Mon-Sat 8pm to 1am
Call: +5411- 4780 5847
Find them on Facebook: Facebook.com/El-Pobre-Luis-51950902634/
Price Range: $$$

Don Julio

This *parrilla* is another restaurant highly recommended by our friends as a top notch experience and a great place to celebrate. It is known to be very busy so better make a reservation or show up early.

Address: Guatemala 4699, Palermo Soho, Buenos Aires
Hours: Daily 12pm to 4pm & 7pm to 1am
Call: +54 114-831-9564
ParrillaDonJulio.com.ar
Price Range: $$$

Patagonia Sur: *A Francis Mallmann Restaurant*

Located in the colorful working class neighborhood of La Boca, this restaurant is an intimate modern/rustic one-table restaurant that looks like it could have been set in a dining room in someone's home. There is no glittering sign on the door, but the humble exterior belies a luxurious experience inside. If you are looking to splurge in Buenos Aires, consider dining at this Francis Mallmann establishment.

Address: Rocha 801, La Boca, Buenos Aires
Hours: Check online or call for reservations.
Call: +54 11-4303-5917
RestaurantePatagoniaSur.com
Price Range: $$$$

Bodegónes

La Tacita

According to our friend Juan Pablo from **AntiGourmet** (see Terroir), this restaurant truly represents a typical *bodegón*. Here you find Spanish-style meals with an Argentine twist. You will also find typical Argentine dishes like *matambre* (pork flank), *bife de chorizo* (sirloin) and *panqueques de dulce de leche* (crepes with dulce de leche). Enjoy!

Address: Avenida Boedo 1595, Boedo, Buenos Aires
Hours: 12pm to 4pm & 8pm to 12am
Call: +54 11 4921-3116
Find them on Facebook: Facebook.com/pages/La-Tacita-De-Boedo/387556801305873
Price Range: $$

La Antigua Torinesa

If you're strolling through San Telmo, this off-the-guidebook locale makes for a great lunch place. An unpretentious storefront, it has a few tables in the back for customers to enjoy homemade specialities from Buenos Aires. Most locals take their food to go. Order the dish of the day for a unique traditional experience.

Address: Avenida Brasil 431, Buenos Aires
Hours: Mon-Fri 9am to 7pm; Sat 9am to 5pm
Call: +54 114-362-3412
ViaResto.com/Ciudad-de-Buenos-Aires/La-Antigua-Torinesa-1571.aspx
Price Range: $

Pizzerias

El Cuartito

El Cuartito is a legendary institution: the long line you will see is an indication of its popularity. They offer pizza by the slice, so you can sample different styles of pizza instead of ordering just one kind. Don't forget to order *fugazetta* and *fainá* to have your pizza the Argentine way. It is an experience not to miss in Buenos Aires.

Address: Talcahuano 937, Buenos Aires
Hours: Daily from 12:30pm to 1am
Call: +54 114-816-1758
Find them on Facebook: Facebook.com/El-Cuartito-78949505516/

Pizzeria Guerrin

This pizzeria has been recommended by locals as a great traditional option to have Argentine-style pizza with *fugazetta* and *fainá*.

Address: Corrientes 1368, Centro, Buenos Aires
Hours: Daily from 11am to 1am
Call: +54 114-371-8141
PizzeriaGuerrin.com

Banchero

Banchero is the pizzeria where the *fugazetta* was born. They have several locations in Buenos Aires. The original location is in La Boca. Go there to taste the original *fugazzeta* in one of the most popular neighborhoods of Buenos Aires.

Address: Suárez 396, Buenos Aires
Hours: Mon-Fri & Sun from 12pm to 4pm & 8pm to 1am; Closed on Sat
Call: +54 114-301-1406
Guiaoleo.com.ar/restaurantes/Banchero-675

Restaurants for Milanesa

El Club de la Milanesa

The modern and rustic design of El Club de la Milanesa makes this restaurant chain stand out in cities across Argentina. They specialize in the preparation of *milanesa* in all its different forms and cooking styles, including over 20 varieties of *sándwich de milanesa*. The unique atmosphere makes this a great option for groups as well.

ElClubDeLaMilanesa.com

Don Ignacio

Don Ignacio is a bodegón, or traditional and homemade style restaurant that crowns itself "El Rey de las Milanesas": the King of Milanesas. They have some of the best *milanesa* in the city. It is an unpretentious restaurant packed with locals from the neighborhood. The decor needs a special mention. Once you walk in, you find yourself surrounded by oldies music record albums from the 50s to the 80s, and the music that goes along with it. Try the *milanesa fugazzeta especial con fritas*. Simply delicious!

Address: Avenida Rivadavia 3439, Caballito, Buenos Aires
Hours: Daily from 10am to 11:30pm
Call: +54 114-861-3133
Find them on Facebook:
Facebook.com/cindyreng

Closed-door restaurants

While we did not experience a "closed-door" restaurant, see **authenticfoodquest.com/argentinabook** for links to AFAR Magazine's **Best Closed Door Restaurants in Buenos Aires** and the Argentina Independent's article on **Top 5 Puertas Cerradas**.

Vegetarian Restaurants

Hierbabuena

This charming and cozy vegetarian restaurant is located near the Parque Lezama in San Telmo. Along with fresh juices and other deliciously fresh foods, they offer some local staples like pizza and pasta with a vegetarian twist. They also have a market next to the restaurant where they sell fresh bread and pastries, fruits and vegetables, as well as organic wines. They serve breakfast, lunch and dinner, with brunch on the weekend. The market is open from Tuesday to Sunday until 9pm.

Address: Avenida Caseros 454, San Telmo, Buenos Aires
Hours: Mon from 9am to 5pm; Tues-Sun from 9am to 12pm
Call: +54 114-362-2542
Hierbabuena.com.ar

Bodhi

Locals come to this buffet lunch spot because the food is fresh and really delicious. You will find a large buffet from which you pick your food and get it weighed by the cashier. If you don't want to pay by the weight you can choose the "all you can eat option" (only on site). It is more expensive, but if you are really hungry it is a great option. Best for takeaway, don't expect a fancy restaurant or a nice seating area, but you can find a spot to sit and eat your lunch on site. They offer *milanesa* made with soy and other local specialities.

Address: Avenida Caseros 454, San Telmo, Buenos Aires
Hours: Daily 11:30am to 3:30pm
Call: +54-114-381-8625
Check out this great review for more information: HappyCow.net/reviews/Bodhi-Buenos-Aires-9908

Explore Further

Guia Oleo

is a website for restaurant recommendations. It is a service similar to Yelp though not as developed and in Spanish only. GuiaOleo.com.ar

For vegetarians, they also list 50 vegetarian options around the city:
http://dixit.guiaoleo.com.ar/cocina-vegetariana-50-opciones-imperdibles-2/

Pick Up The Fork

This is a fantastic guide put together by Allie Lazar, with restaurant and market recommendations for Buenos Aires:
PickUpTheFork.com

AntiGourmet

For the best traditional restaurant guide or bodegones, see the guide put together at **AntiGourmet.com.ar** (in Spanish only).

Happy Cow

You will find nearly 90 vegetarian listings in English:
HappyCow.net/South_America/Argentina/Buenos_Aires/

Bares Notables

Distinguished by the city of Buenos Aires for their historical or cultural significance, the 73 *bares notables*, "notable bars," are an official part of the heritage of Buenos Aires. On your travels, step back into time and enjoy a *media tarde* here before dinner. Listed below are five *bares notables* we recommend. For a full listing, please see this link from the City of Buenos Aires: BuenosAires.gob.ar/culturadecafe/bares.

Bar El Federal

Bar El Federal is the second oldest bar in the city, located in San Telmo. Come here to mix with locals and tourists alike and appreciate a *cafe con leche con tostadas* (coffee and toasted sandwiches) or a *cerveza artesanale* (craft beer).

Address: Carlos Calvo, 599, Buenos Aires
Hours: Daily from 8am to 12am
Call: +54 114-300-4313
BarelFederal.com.ar/

La Biela

La Biela is located across Recoleta cemetery where Eva Peron, the First Lady of Argentina, was buried in the 1950s. Here you can sit next to the statue of Jorge Luis Borges, the famous Argentine poet. This bar has an old fashioned and traditional atmosphere, and of course, they serve the *Imperial*, one of the premium beers of Argentina.

Address: Avenida Presidente Manuel Quintana 596, Recoleta Buenos Aires
Hours: Daily from 7am to 2am
Call: +54 114-804-0449
LaBiela.com

Café Tortoni

Watch live tango under the beautiful stained glass ceiling and choose from classic dishes on the menu at the most visited café in Buenos Aires. This historical *porteños* café (for Buenos Aires locals) with its French-inspired architecture is a cultural landmark.

Address: Avenida de Mayo 825, Buenos Aires
Hours: Mon to Sun from 8am to 1am
Call: +54 114-342-4328
CafeTortoni.com.ar/en/

Café La Poesia

This bares notable is a quaint historical café in the neighborhood of San Telmo. They have a large food menu with *media tarde* specials and artisanal beer.

Address: Chile 502, San Telmo, Buenos Aires, Argentina.
Hours: Daily from 8am to 1am
Call: +54 114-300-7340
CafeLaPoesia.com.ar

Bar Seddon

This classic bar in San Telmo is located a few blocks from Café la Poesia. This is one of the few bares notables that is opened until 4am, and they accept credit cards here. The menu is limited but you will find a few Argentine staples.

Address: Defensa 695, San Telmo, Buenos Aires, Argentina
Hours: Tues-Fri, 10am to 4am; Sat from 6pm to 4am
Call: +54 114-342-3700
Find them on Facebook:
Facebook.com/BarSeddon

STREET FOOD VENDORS

There are two main areas to find street food in Buenos Aires. One is in Puerto Madero along the Reserva Costanera Sur (Ecological Reserve). Here you will find many *parrilla* trucks selling *choripán, bondiola* and *lomito*. It is a nice stop to make after visiting the Reserva.

The second place to get street food in Buenos Aires is near Jorge Newbery Airport on Avenida Costanera Rafael Obligado, near what is popularly known as the Costanera

Norte. Here you will find arguably the best *choripán* in town.

You can also find a *pancho* in Retiro, the main bus and train station of Buenos Aires. During street fairs and farmers markets, you will find some street vendors selling *garrapiñadas* and fast food sandwiches.

UNIQUE CULINARY EXPERIENCES

Cooking Classes

While we did not have the chance to take cooking classes in Buenos Aires. These two classes are highly recommended by locals.

Tierra Negra

Manuel is a professional chef, who teaches travelers how to cook the authentic dishes from Argentina in small groups using local ingredients.

Where: Palermo Hollywood, Buenos Aires
When: Tues & Thurs from 6pm to 9pm, Wed & Sat from 10am to 1pm
Email: info@tierranegragourmet.com
TierraNegraGourmet.com

Argentine Cooking Classes

Norma offers cooking classes in English and Spanish at her home for small groups, and she can also accommodate private groups and vegetarians as well.

Where: Belgrano, Buenos Aires.
When: Tues & Sat from 11am to 2pm
Call: +54 154-470-2267
Email: normasoued@gmail.com
ArgentineCookingClasses2.com

Food Tours

Parrilla Tour

If you are in Buenos Aires and short on time, take a food tour with Parrilla Tour. This is an excellent company that will allow you to discover the city through delicious and traditional foods. In small intimate settings with knowledgeable English speaking guides, you will eat where the locals eat and discover the secret gems in the city. You can read more about the tour through San Telmo at authenticfoodquest.com/argentinabook. We enjoyed this tour for the authenticity of the food and places. This tour was booked for us by **Bsas4u Tours & Activities in Buenos Aires**. They also propose other local activities that might be of interest to you as well.

Where: Tour offered in Palermo & San Telmo
Tours on: Mon, Tues Wed, Fri & Sat at 12pm, with an additional tour on Tues at 7:30pm. Tours last about 2.5 hours.
Discount code: Get your discount code for a food tour at authenticfoodquest.com/argentinabook

Pick Up The Fork

Chicago expat Allie Lazar is a culinary expert in Buenos Aires. She specializes in "the anti-tour:" fully customizable, off-the-beaten-path food itineraries. She takes foodies on tours through traditional marketplaces, hidden cafés, and hole-in-the-wall eateries. Her **website** provides tons of additional information on the food scene in Buenos Aires.

Email: feedme@pickupthefork.com
PickUpTheFork.com

Fuudis

Co-founded by Maria (an Argentine) and Anna (originally from Australia), Fuudis offers gourmet tours in the city. They create food experiences combining gastronomy, art and social gathering. They offer lunch and dinner tours, which are truly an excuse to socialize the Argentine way, visit three restaurants in one outing. They also offer an *Aperitour* where you get to visit bars in Buenos Aires and sample drinks and tapas.

Where: San Telmo, Buenos Aires
Email: hola@fuudis.com

Food Festivals
Feria de Mataderos

For those interested in Gaucho culture, check out the Feria de Mataderos which is held every Sunday (March through December). It takes place in Barrio Matadores which is a short ride away from the center of Buenos Aires. While it is a gaucho fair, it is one of the best places for Argentine street food. Here you can sample the *choripán* (grilled sausages) or *pancho* (hot dogs) and even some of the regional specialities like *locro*, *tamales*, *humitas* and *empanadas*.

When: Every Sun from March to December
Where: Avenida de los Corrales 6500, Mataderos, Buenos Aires.
FeriaDeMataderos.com.ar

Semana de Bodegones

This week is dedicated to celebrating the bodegones restaurants in Buenos Aires. For one week, fifty bodegones offer promotional menus to invite people to discover their gastronomy.

When: Second week of September
Where: Buenos Aires
Find them on Facebook: Facebook.com/SemanaDeLosBodegones/

Feria Masticar: CHEW Fair

Here you can travel the globe through food from the Caribbean to the Amalfi coast with just one bite. This immensely popular and growing food festival is not to be missed. Launched in 2012, the festival has more than 50 of the country's best restaurants offer a sample of their menus at low prices. The dishes offered are classics as well as reinterpretations of traditional recipes.

While the festival is called "Chew", there is an abundant supply of wines. Wine bars located throughout the festival pair foods with Argentine wines. Vegetarians, you will not be disappointed. Each of the restaurants featured offer a vegetarian option. Go hungry and open yourself up to new tastes and flavors.

When: Dates vary for this annual festival.
Where: Buenos Aires
FeriaMasticar.com.ar

Buenos Aires Food Week

This gastronomic event is organized over a two week period in Buenos Aires. It features more than 50 restaurants that offer a fixed three course menu at a promotional price. It is a great way to discover some of the best restaurants of the capital.

When: September
Where: Buenos Aires
BAFoodWeek.com
Find them on Facebook:
Facebook.com/BAFoodWeek

Raíz Festival de la Gastronomía

Argentina's largest food festival is the Raíz Festival de la Gastronomía. The festival features traditional Argentine cooking methods, the different **empanadas** styles from across the country, the diversity of immigrant cultures, wine tastings and more. In 2015, the organizers put an emphasis on sustainable and healthier foods with the mini 'ECO festival'. Vegan cuisine, organic food and gluten-free options were all available.

When: First week of October
Where: Tecnópolis exhibition park, Buenos Aires
FestivalRaiz.com

Fiesta Nacional de la Pasta Casera

Tucked in the town of General Las Heras, about an hour and twenty minutes (by car) southwest of Buenos Aires, this festival of National Homemade Pasta is held during the first half of April. The origin of the festival is associated with the famous pasta-making machine called Pastalinda, created by a local entrepreneur in the mid-twentieth century. The event is a celebration of a social and cultural tradition linked with the familiar ritual of making homemade pasta. You will find gastronomic exhibitions and cooking classes by renowned chefs as well as musical shows and craft fairs.

When: First half of April
Where: General Las Heras
Find them on Facebook: Facebook.com/muniglh

Fiesta de la Picada y la Cerveza Artesanal

Over two days, this festival celebrates artisanal beers of Argentina with over 40 craft breweries represented from across the country. There is a musical show as well as stands with cheese and cured meat from the region, called *picada*. Located an hour outside of Buenos Aires in the town of Uribelarrea, this festival is worth the visit.

When: Two days in the first half of October
Where: Uribelarrea
Find them on Facebook: Facebook.com/FiestaDeLaPicadaY LaCervezaArtesanal

More Festivals

For more information about other festivals in Buenos Aires, check the yearly calendar at EverFest: **EverFest.com/ar/buenos-aires-festivals**

TANDIL

Located southeast of Buenos Aires is the Pampas region famous for its grass fed cattle. Here you can enjoy a stay in an *estancia* and live the *gaucho* life!

Estancias are essentially ranches that play a significant role in the history, culture and economy of Argentina. Dating back to the 17th and 18th centuries, these extensive farms in the Pampas have raised the cattle and grains that have made Argentina one of the biggest meat and grain producers in the world, and today Tandil is known for its cheese, cured meats and salami. It is a great place to have an **asado**, Argentina's national dish, at a local **parrilla** or at an *estancia*.

FOOD STORES

The Big Stores
Supermercado Monarca

This is a great grocery store in the region. They have a bakery on site with fresh and local specialities. You will also find your usual grocery items, fruits and vegetables.

Address: Avenida Colón 1050, Tandil
Hours: Daily from 9am to 1:30pm & 5pm to 9pm
Call: +54 249-443-5034
Find them on Facebook: Facebook.com/Supermercados-Monarca-206284989497589/

Local Specialty Stores
Verdulería
Central Tandil

This store distributes vegetables and fruits across the region. They are now open to the public, selling their produce at attractive prices.

Address: Avenida Ricardo Balbín 1150, 7000 Tandil
Call: +54 249-422-0880
Hours: Mon-Fri, 8am to 8pm; Sun from 9am to 1pm. Closed on Sat.

Cheese and cured meat store
Epoca de Quesos

Conveniently located couple blocks from the center of town, this is (obviously by its Spanish name) first and foremost a cheese store. Additionally, it offers cured meat and other delicacies from the region. The best part is their *picadas* where they serve you local cheese with Argentine wine.

Address: 14 de Julio 604 esq. San Martin., Tandil
Hours: Daily from 9am to 11pm; closed on Wednesdays in the winter.
Call: +54 249 444-8750
EpocaDeQuesos.com

RESTAURANTS

Tandil is known for its beef and you will find many *parrilla* restaurants serving grilled and cured meat. The restaurants are mostly located downtown next to the pedestrian area. Here are a few addresses given to us by locals. Feel free to give them a try or stroll around downtown and find a restaurant to your taste.

Parrilla El Trebol

Address: Mitre 298 y 14 de julio, Tandil, Argentina
Hours: Mon-Sat from 12pm to 3pm & 8:30pm to 12am; except Sun 12pm to 3pm
Call: +54 249-444-2333
ComercialTandil.com.ar/empresas/parrilla-eltrebol/index.htm#_=_
Price Range: $$

Parrilla El Criollo

Address: Rodriguez 650
Hours: Mon-Fri from 12pm to 3pm & 8pm to 12am
Call: +54 229-342-5660
VivoTandil.com/donde-comer-el-criollo-parrilla-84.html
Price Range: $$

Parrilla La Pulperia
Address: Avenida Estrada 1395, Tandil, Argentina
Hours: Daily from 8pm to 1am
Call: +54 229-343-6699

Find them on Facebook: Facebook.com/Parrilla-La-Pulper%C3%ADa-Tandil-143915708996292/
Price Range: $$

Estancia Hostería Ave Maria

Recommended to us by locals, Ave Maria is a charming bed and breakfast located fifteen minutes from Tandil. They propose horseback riding to visit the region. They serve homemade breakfast and regional cuisine for lunch and dinner.

Address: Paraje La Porteña, Circuito Turístico, Tandil, Argentina.
Hours: Check on site for dining hours. Open all year round.
Call: +54 249-442-2843
AveMariaTandil.com
Price Range: $$$

The Wine Regions
MENDOZA

Nestled under the Andes, Argentina's wine capital of Mendoza is a desert town, though it doesn't look like one with its palm trees and fountains. You can see water flowing from the mountain peaks to the *acequais*, irrigation ditches, that run beside the main roads in the city. A favorable climate combined with the high altitude and its irrigation system makes Mendoza an ideal region for producing wine and growing local fruits and vegetables.

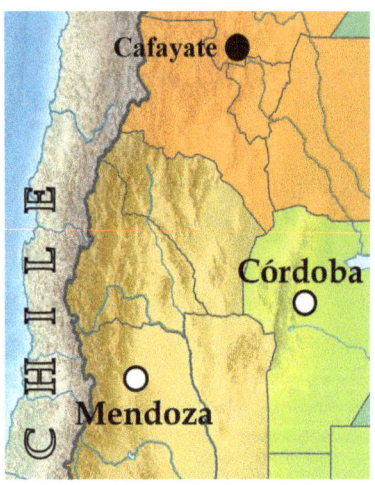

The Wine Regions, based on B1mbo work

The city itself has wide avenues, lots of restaurants and cafes on pedestrian streets and the famous Parque General San Martin (San Martin Park). Here you will find many *bodegas* or wineries to enjoy the famous Malbec and great local cuisine.

Besides being the largest producer of Malbec, Mendoza is also the 4th largest city in Argentina with close proximity to Santiago, Chile and Aconcagua, the highest mountain peak outside of Asia at 6,961 meters (22,800 ft).

The splendid view of the Andes and the laid back pace makes it easy to get captivated by the city.

FARMERS MARKETS

Mercado Central

This market is located in downtown Mendoza near the pedestrian streets. You will find many types of vendors from fruits and vegetables, to cheese, bread, meat and fish. There is also a section of the market dedicated to vendors selling local specialities: *empanadas*, *tortas*, *facturas* and more. The stores within the market close for the *siesta* at midday. There is a food court where restaurants stay open during lunch time. You will find basic food such as pasta, *milanesa*, *parrilla*, and more.

Address: Las Heras 300, Mendoza
Hours: Mon-Sat from 8am to 1pm & 4pm to 9pm
Link to website: authenticfoodquest.com/argentinabook

Mercado de Guaymallen

This important farmers market is used by local restaurants and chefs. It is located on the east side of Mendoza, on the outskirts of the city. It is an important market for fruits and vegetables as well as related products (olive oil, bread etc.).

Address: Sarmiento 1155, Mendoza
Hours: Mon-Fri, 8am to 1pm & 4pm to 9pm; Sat from 8am to 1pm
MercadoDeGuaymallen.hol.es/

FOOD STORES

The Big Stores

Carrefour

Carrefour has several locations in Mendoza including Carrefour Market. The largest location is conveniently located near the light rail station in downtown Mendoza. This is a large supermarket where you will find everything you need. Farmers markets and speciality stores are your best bet for more local products.

Address: Avenida Belgrano 1421, Mendoza
Hours: Mon-Sat, 8:30am to 10pm; Sun 9am-10pm
Carrefour.com.ar

Local Specialty Stores

Kiosko

For fruits and vegetables, besides the farmers market, you will find small kiosks in the street that offer a selection of a few fruits and vegetables. There are several on Avenida Belgrano.

Location 1: Corner of Belgrano & Avenida Juan B Justo
Location 2: Corner of Av. Belgrano & Avenida Colon

Feria La Quinta

This is a small verdulería located on the northwest side of town. They have a limited selection of fresh produce but the prices are attractively low.

Address: Avenida Juan B. Justo 438, Mendoza
Hours: Daily from 9am to 9:30pm (check hours with vendors during siesta)

THE WINE REGIONS

Pasta Stores
La Veneciana

This artisanal store offers delicious pasta from the famous Argentine *sorrentinos* to fettucine. You will also find delicious sauces to make a full meal with the pasta of your choice. They also have *empanadas*, bread and pastries for sale. They have several locations listed with hours on their website. We mention here the main location downtown Mendoza.

Address: Avenida San Martín 895, Mendoza
Hours: Daily from 8am to 10pm
La-Vene.com

Heladerías (Ice-cream Stores)
Heladería Perrin

This traditional ice-cream store has been a corner fixture in Mendoza for over 66 years. Today, it is still owned by the same family. Mendocinos stop here with their family on Sunday afternoon. You will find many flavors to choose from. They also serve breakfast.

Address: Sarmiento 799, Mendoza
Hours: Daily from 10am to 2am, Fri & Sat closes at 3am
Call: +54 261 425-7624
Find them on Facebook: Facebook.com/FamigliaPerinHelados

RESTAURANTS

Mariá Antonieta

Vanina Chimeno, chef and owner of Mariá Antonieta, creates traditional and popular dishes with seasonal ingredients from the region. Try the *hamburguesa María Antonieta*, a classic and exquisite option (the bread is made fresh at the restaurant). It is open for breakfast, lunch and dinner. The menu changes by season and you may find the local speciality *tomatican* or other local dishes depending of the season. Ask the staff to guide you when making your choice. The restaurant has a nice feel with the open kitchen and bistro decor.

Address: Belgrano 1069, Mendoza
Hours: Mon-Fri, 8am to 12pm; Sat 9am to 12pm; Sun 10am to 5pm
Call: +54 261-420-4322
MariaAntonietaResto.com.ar
Price Range: $$

Siete Cocinas

The concept at this restaurant is to offer a menu with dishes from four to seven different regions of Argentina, and thus Siete Cocinas was recommended to us by several Argentines. They offer fine regional cuisine that allows you to travel through food.

Address: Avenue Bartolome Mitre 794, 5500 Capital, Mendoza
Hours: Mon-Sat from 8:30pm to 11pm
Call: +54 261-423-8823
SieteCocinas.com.ar
Price Range: $$$

1884

This iconic Francis Mallmann *parrilla* is located in the Bodega Escorihuela winery in Mendoza. The restaurant uses the open-fire approach to cooking meat. Ranked in the **World Best Latin American Restaurants**, it is a must try

if you want to splurge on one night in Mendoza.
Address: Belgrano 1188, Godoy Cruz, Mendoza, Argentina
Hours: Daily from 8pm to 12pm
Call: +54 261-424-3336/424-2698
1884restaurante.com.ar
Price Range: $$$$

Nutri Verde Vegetariano

Gladys runs this casual vegetarian restaurant that offers a salad and hot buffet. You can choose the all-you-can-eat option or order your food by weight. In any case, it is very reasonably priced and tasty. Locals are lining up before the opening hours which is always a good sign. Gladys makes *tomaticán*, the local tomato speciality, as well as *empanada de choclo* and other vegetarian preparations. Check the address as they were looking to move to a bigger place due to their success!
Address: General Paz 328, Mendoza
Hours: Daily from 12:30pm to 3:30pm
Call: +54-261-423-4042
Find more information: HappyCow.net/reviews/nutri-verde-mendoza-20641
Price Range: $

Wine Not?

This wine bar is new in Mendoza and it opened in early 2016. You can taste different wines before (and after) visiting the wineries and make your choice on which one to tour. You can also enjoy *empanadas* and cheese plates to go with the wines. A gem in Mendoza!
Address: 25 de Mayo 917, Mendoza
Hours: Sat & Sun 5pm to 11pm
Information: +54-261-565-8970
WineNotMendoza.com
Price Range: $

You will also find additional restaurants in the winery section.

UNIQUE CULINARY EXPERIENCES

Cooking Classes

Cristina Brino

Cristina offers cooking classes at **Finca Adalgisa**, a small winery and boutique hotel located about half hour (by car) from Mendoza. Cristina teaches how to prepare *empanadas*, rib eye steak with a *chimichurri* sauce and caramelized fruit. She uses the traditional clay oven or a *parrilla* with open fire. Tour and wine tasting are also available at the winery.
Where: Finca Adalgisa Winery, Pueyrredón 2222, Chacras de Coria, Mendoza, Argentina
When: Check with the winery for availability.
Call: +54 261-613-1771
CristinaBrino.com.ar

Asado Cooking Class

If you have a desire to learn how to make an *asado* or barbecue like the Argentines, this is your class. Mauricio will teach you the fine techniques to make a perfect wood fire and cook meat on a *parrilla* the traditional way.
Where: Mauricio´s house in Mendoza; private transportation provided from hotel.
When: Mon-Sat, starts at 11am
Email: maucamen@hotmail.com
AsadoCookingClassMendoza.com

More and more wineries offer cooking classes along with wine tasting. Look for wineries that are offering classes in the wineries and wine tasting section.

Food Tours

Eat Mendoza

Eat Mendoza offers food tours that have you taste traditional foods and great wine. This tour allows you to discover local restaurants and learn about the cuisine and culture of Mendoza.

Tours on: Tues & Fri from 7:30pm, lasts 2.5-3 hours
Email: info@eatmendoza.com
EatMendoza.com

Villavicencio Natural Reserve Tour

Villavicencio is the most widely sold brand of mineral water in the country. It comes from Villavicencio Natural Reserve, located about 50 km (30 mi) north of Mendoza. The only way to visit Villavicencio is to take a tour. Book one from one of the many agencies in downtown Mendoza.

Address: Villavicencio Natural Reserve, Mendoza
Hours: Wed-Fri from 9:30am to 6:30pm (last visit at 5:30pm); Sat & Sun from 9:30am to 7pm (last visit at 6pm). Entrance fee: ARS120, (AR80 for Argentine resident).
MVillavicencio.com.ar

Farm Tours

Olive Oil Farm Tours

The region of Maipú which is about 15 km (9 mi) southeast of Mendoza is one of the largest olive oil producing regions of Argentina. You will find several tours offered to visit *olivicolas* (olive oil factories) across the region. Some of the tours are free and include an olive oil tasting, while some might require a minimum entrance fee. Check the *olivicola* website or contact them for more information on their tours and tastings.

Some of the olive farms are accessible by local bus G10 #182 (about one hour from the center of Mendoza to the bus stop located at the crossing of La Rioja and Catamarca). The following *Magazine Gourmet* article includes a directory of dozens of olive farms in the region: **MagazineGourmet.com/restaurantes/olivicolas**.

Highlighted below are the *olivicolas* we visited and some that were recommended by locals.

Pasrai

The Pasrai *olivicola* was established in 1920. It is located near the Bodega Cecchin (organic wines) in Maipú. They offer free tours of the manufacturing process as well as a tasting of a variety of olive oils. The tour is complimentary and nicely organized. Highly recommended if you want to learn about the olive oil processing in the region and enjoy the tasting on your way to the wineries.

Address: Ozami Sur 1957, Maipú, Mendoza
Hours: Daily from 10am to 12:30pm & 3pm to 6:30pm
Call: +54 261-154-7076
Pasrai.com.ar

Olivicola Simone

This is a small and intimate family-owned olive oil factory; the son gives the tours, which start with a tasting of the four types of oil sold by the *olivicola*, as well as sampling green and black olives. They do not grow their own olives, but they get them from long standing growers. Most of the tour information is given via video and only in Spanish; while not the most interesting experience, it does provide another perspective on olive oils in Mendoza.

Address: Ozami Sur 1553, Maipú, Mendoza, Argentina.

Hours: Mon-Sat, 9am to 1pm & 4pm to 8pm; Sun from 10:30am to 1pm.
Entrance fee: ARS 50.
Call: +54 261-481-1151
OlivicolaSimone.com

Maguay

This is a family-run olive farm located near the two places above. Check their hours as they were closed when we were looking to visit after stopping by the other nearby olive oil farms.

Address: Ozami Sur 1491, Maipú, Mendoza
Hours: Mon-Sat from 9am to 1pm & 4pm to 7pm; Sun 10:30am to 1pm. Contact Maguay ahead for visit hours & fees.
Call: +54 261-497-2632
Maguay.com.ar

Laur

The first olive farm of Mendoza is still decorated with old machinery, now kept in a museum among the olive groves. Laur was founded by Francisco Laur, a French immigrant, at the beginning of the 1900s. He was a pioneer in the cultivation of olive trees in Mendoza as well as the production of extra virgin olive oil. A tour of the farm includes a visit of the olive trees, the museum with the old machinery, the current production area and the added vinegar production area. The tour ends with a tasting of the different oils and vinegar.

Address: Videla aranda 2850, Cruz de Piedra, Maipú, Mendoza
Hours: Daily from 10:30am to 6:30pm
Entrance fee: ARS50
Call: +54 261-499-0716
OlvLaur.com/en

Familia Zuccardi

This is an olive oil farm that is mainly known for its wine. To get more information on this winery and olive oil farm please read the section on **Maipú Valley Winery Visits**.

Winery Tours, Tastings, and Cooking Classes

The Three Wine Valleys of Mendoza

Mendoza has over 1,500 wineries spread out in three main wine valleys: **Maipu Valley, Luján de Cuyo Valley and Uco Valley.** There is quite a bit of distance between them; Uco Valley is the furthest from Mendoza, with a minimum one hour drive. Keep in mind that you cannot drink and drive!

However you choose to experience Mendoza, be very clear on what kind of experience you are seeking.

- For a light and fun experience close to Mendoza that won't break the bank or require reservations ahead of time, choose **Maipú Valley**. You will be able to cover more ground in less time and visit several wineries in a day.

- For an in-depth experience with quality wine, plan your trip around the **Luján de Cuyo** and **Uco** Valleys.

- If you are looking for beautiful landscape and spectacular views, **Uco Valley** is for you.

- If you are pressed for time, skip Uco Valley (where the wineries are more spread out) and stay around the more compact **Luján de Cuyo**.

For more information about the valleys and their characteristics, check out **BodegaArgento.com/en**. This winery uses grapes from across the Mendoza region, and includes detailed information about soil types, rainfall and varietals in each area; an excellent resource to learn more about the *terroir* of the wines.

Once you are clear on what you want, you will be able to find a suitable way to visit the wineries. Here are our tips to make the most of your Mendoza wine experience:

10 TIPS TO MAKE THE MOST OF YOUR WINERY VISITS IN MENDOZA

1. Orient yourself at the **Winenot?** Wine bar. Taste the offerings from different vineyards to decide which wineries you would like to visit.
2. Choose which valley you want to visit: Maipú, Luján de Cuyo or Uco Valley. Plan your day in one valley at a time.
3. Make reservations ahead for most of the wineries and restaurants: at least one to two days in advance is required. As you plan your visits, keep in mind that the tours generally last from 45 min to 1.5 hours.
4. Plan your visit between Monday and Friday. Weekends are usually slow and most of the wineries are closed.
5. Get explicit directions prior to your winery visit. Even with a GPS system, not all wineries are well marked.
6. Even better, hire a driver so that you can safely savor the wines, and take in the magnificent views.
7. Limit your visit to three to four wineries per day, especially if you are stopping for lunch. Most of the wineries close early in the evening.
8. Have plenty of Argentine pesos handy as most wineries do not accept credit cards.
9. Take advantage of the unique opportunity to meet the winery owners and winemakers themselves at the wineries. Ask them as many questions as you like. They enjoy sharing their knowledge and their stories.
10. Don't like to plan? Use one of the many tour agencies in Mendoza. Or borrow one of the sample itineraries at **ExperienceMendoza.com/en/itineraries**. They have a three day plan to visit all the valleys, or a one day plan for each of Luján de Cuyo and Uco Valleys.

Maipú Valley

Maipú Valley is the closest valley to Mendoza. Maipú is a small town 15 km (9 mi) southeast of Mendoza packed with wineries and olive oil farms. It is easy to hit several wineries here in one day. Renting a bicycle to move from winery to winery is a popular activity in this region: you can get to this valley by public transportation and then rent a bike to hop from winery to winery. From downtown Mendoza, take the bus G10- #171/#172/#173 to the intersection of La Rioja and Catamarca in Maipú. Get off at Coquimbito and rent bikes from either **Hugo Bikes** or **Coco Bikes**. Visit **authenticfoodquest.com/argentinabook** for links to websites.

Mevi

Enjoy a beautiful view of the Andes on the Mevi patio, while sampling their wines with cheese and crackers. This small boutique winery is located in Maipú Valley and is a short bus ride away from Mendoza. This family-owned *bodega* is conveniently located next to other wineries so you can hit a couple wineries all within walking distance.
Address: Carril Perito Moreno 1751, Coquimbito, Maipú
Hours: Mon-Sat, 11am to 7pm
Call: +54 261-481-4747 / 497-2600
FincaMevi.com.ar

Familia Cecchin

This family-owned vineyard dates back from 1959, and is one of the few wineries producing organic wines. The tour includes visiting the vineyard and the tasting. If you buy a bottle of wine the tasting is included.
Address: Manuel A. Saenz 626, Maipú
Hours: Mon-Sat, 11am to 7pm
Call: +54 261-497-6707
FamiliaCecchin.com.ar

Tempus Alba Restaurant & Winery *Cooking classes offered*

Rooftop views of the Andes are a delicious pairing with the wine tasting menu and lunch offered at Tempus Alba. Within walking distance to Mevi, this winery has a self guided tour, although you can wait for the guided visit. They also offer cooking classes. Check directly with Tempus Alba for more information.
Address: Carril Perito Moreno 572, Coquimbito, Maipú
Hours: Mon-Fri, 10:30am to 6pm
Call: +54 261-481-3501
TempusAlba.com

Familia Zuccardi Restaurant & Winery *Cooking classes offered - Olive oil farm*

This organic winery was recommended to us by our Airbnb hosts in Buenos Aires. They produce gourmet olive oil and wines. You can tour their olive oil mill and also the winery. Tasting, cooking classes and lunch is offered as well.
Address: Ruta Prov 33 km 7,5, Maipú
Hours: Mon-Sat, 9am to 6pm; Sun from 10am to 5pm
Call: +54 261-441-0000
FamiliaZuccardi.com

Rutini Wines & Bodega La Rural Winery *Wine Museum*

Rutini Wines offers tours through its historic winery Bodega La Rural, and the Museo del Vino (Wine Museum). Since its foundation in 1885, Bodega La Rural has been noted for the quality of its wine, and the Museo del Vino is one of the most important and unique wine museums in the Americas.
Address: Montecaseros 2625, Coquimbito, Maipú
Hours: Mon-Sat, 9am to 1pm & 2pm to 5pm
Call: +54 261-520-7666
RutiniWines.com

Trapiche

This is the largest winery in Mendoza and Trapiche exports its wines to more than 80 countries in the world. Trapiche is well-known for its Malbec in the USA. If you are interested in visiting a large winery in a nicely renovated *bodega*, this is a great choice.
Address: Nueva Mayorga s/n 5513, Maipú
Hours: Mon-Fri, 9am to 5pm; Sat & Sun from 10am to 3pm
Call: +54-261-520-7666
Trapiche.com.ar in country or
TrapicheWines-USA.com from the U.S.

Luján de Cuyo

Luján de Cuyo is known as Malbec Land, and was the first region to be a "designation of origin" (AOC) for Malbec in 1993.

Luján de Cuyo is not as accessible as Maipú to tour the wineries. You can still access the region by bus, though the wineries are further apart. You will need to rely on taxis to move from one winery to another.

The best would be to hire a driver or book a tour from the numerous agencies in downtown Mendoza. You can also rent a car (though not recommended unless you have a designated driver—remember Argentina has a zero tolerance policy with drinking and driving).

Book the **Bus Vitivinocola** for half or full day itineraries. Check their website for pricing information (BusVitivinicola.com/ingles). Most of the wineries highlighted below were recommended to us by locals.

Dominio del Plata Restaurant — *Cooking classes offered*

Owner Susana Balbo will welcome you into her home for lunch: a menu that walks you through five steps of regional cuisine, paired with five premium wines, all with the backdrop of the amazing Andes. Not only is this winery operated by the most famous female winemaker and consultant of Argentina, but she is also a pioneer in exporting wines to USA and Brazil.

Address: Cochabamba 7801 Agrelo, Luján de Cuyo
Hours: Mon-Fri, 9am to 3pm
Call: +54 261-498-9200
En.SusanaBalboWines.com.ar

Catena Zapata

Nicola Zapata was one of the pioneers from Italy who settled in Argentina and planted his first Malbec vineyard in 1902. Today, the *bodega* is still run by the Catena family. The Catena wines are some of the most renowned in the region.

Address: J. Cobos, 5509 Luján de Cuyo, Mendoza
Hours: Mon-Fri, 9am to 6pm; Sat from 9am to 2pm
Call: +54 262-245-1579
CatenaWines.com/

Pulenta Estate

Pulenta Estate is run by one of the most important families in the wine industry of Argentina. The owners love wine and cars in equal measure; their wine cellar doubles as a car engine exhibition. Located south from Luyan de Cuyo, you will enjoy nice wines with a great view of the Andes.

Address: Ruta Provincial 86 KM 6.5, Alto Agrelo, 5509 Luján de Cuyo, Mendoza
Hours: Mon-Fri, 9am to 5pm; Sat from 9am to 1pm
Call: +54 261-507-6426
PulentaEstate.com/en

Viña Cobos

Bodega Viña Cobos is a modern winery located south of Luján de Cuyo. You will find excellent wines at this winery, which is consistently rated for its premium wines. Be sure to make reservations ahead of time.

Address: Costa Flores s/n y Ruta 7, Perdriel, 5509 Luján de Cuyo, Mendoza
Hours: Mon-Fri, 9am to 5pm; Sat from 9am to 1pm
Call: +54 261-674-6689
VinaCobos.com/en

Norton Restaurant La Vid
Wine harvesting & winemaking classes - Cooking classes offered

Norton is one of the most recognizable Malbec wines in the USA. It is also one of the most productive wineries of the region. Norton offers visits and wine tastings without reservations. You can also stay for lunch in their Restaurant La Vid to prolong your experience. Norton also offers additional activities such as cooking classes, harvesting and farming activities, and winemaking class. Reserve ahead of time for these activities.

Address: Ruta Provincial 15 km 23,5, 5509 Perdriel, Mendoza
Hours: Daily from 9am to 6pm
Call: +54 261-490-9700
Norton.com.ar

Uco Valley

Uco Valley is one of the world's highest wine growing regions, with over 80,000 hectares planted between 3,000 ft and 3,900 ft. Wines from grapes grown at this altitude are said to be among the best that Mendoza has to offer.

Uco Valley is not readily accessible by public transportation. The best option would be to hire a driver or book a tour from the numerous agencies in downtown Mendoza. If you have a designated driver, you can rent a car—as mentioned previously, Argentina has a zero tolerance policy with drinking and driving.

Bus Vitivinocola offers full day itineraries for the Uco Valley. Check their website for the most recent pricing (**BusVitivinicola.com/ingles**). Most of the wineries highlighted below were recommended to us by locals.

The Vines of Mendoza Resort & Spa
Winemaking workshops

This boutique and culinary resort is located about 1.5 hours from Mendoza. The Vines of Mendoza's Uco Valley Winery offers unique workshops for barrel tasting, blending your own wines, and even seeing barrel fermentation in action. You can take tours which can be customized to the needs of your group. The Vines Resort offers breathtaking views of the Andes mountains and great patio to sip your wine, surrounded by the vineyards it came from. They make more than 300 unique vintages each year and you can even purchase your own parcel of vines.

Address: Ruta 94, km 11, 5565 Tunuyán, Uco Valley, Mendoza
Hours: Daily from 10am to 6pm; by reservation only
Call: +54 261-469-1909
VinesOfMendoza.com

Siete Fuegos Restaurant
Cooking Classes Offered

Siete Fuegos or "Seven Fires" by Francis Mallmann is the signature restaurant at The Vines Resort & Spa. Experience the open flame cooking techniques of the *parrilla* and savor the rustic, fiery flavors of specialities like nine-hour slow-grilled rib eye, cast-iron baked salt-encrusted salmon, grilled seasonal fruits and more. You can also book a cooking class or learn how to make your own wine. See article about our incredible cooking class experience at Siete Fuegos titled "**Francis Mallmann and the Seven Fires**" at authenticfoodquest.com/argentinabook.

Address: The Vines Resort & Spa, Ruta 94, km 11, 5565 Tunuyan, Uco Valley, Mendoza
Hours: Daily from 12:30pm to 12am
Call: +54 261-461-3910
VinesResort&Spa.com

Gimenez Riili

Conveniently located next to The Vines of Mendoza. Gimenez Riili is a family-run and boutique winery. Stop here for lunch and sample their signature wines.

Address: Ruta 94 Km 8 Camino al Manzano Histórico, Tunuyán - Mendoza, 5560 Vista Flores, Mendoza
Hours: Daily from 10am to 5pm (call for reservations)
Call: +54 261-498-7863
GimenezRiili.com

La Azul

This is one of the smallest wineries in Mendoza. They offer personalized and small group visits for an intimate experience. Don't forget to taste their Gran Reserva blend.

Address: San Martín 1131, Tunuyán, Mendoza
Hours: Check directly with the bodega for reservations
Call: +54-262-242-3593
BodegaLaAzul.com/ingles

O. Fournier Urban Restaurant

This *bodega* has a very interesting modern architecture worth visiting for its impressive cellars. Their wines are consistently highly rated. This is a great place to sip, relax, and enjoy a delicious lunch in their sumptuous dining room.

Address: Calle Los Indios s/n, 5567 La Consulta, Mendoza
Hours: Daily from 9am to 6pm
Call: +54-261-467-1021
OFournier.com

Salentein Restaurant Killka

This unique *bodega* is not only devoted to the art of making wines; it also includes art galleries. The atrium doubles as a classical concert room. This winery is a cultural experience not to be missed.

Address: Ruta 89 s/n, 5560 Los Arboles, Mendoza
Hours: Mon-Sat, 9am to 1pm & 2pm to 5pm
Call: +54 262-242-9500
BodegaSalentein.com/en

Notable places to eat outside the wineries

YA-CE Lomitería

If you want something more down to earth than the pricey and gourmet lunch at the wineries, head over to YA-CE and order one of their delicious *lomitos* (typical Argentine sirloin steak sandwich).

Address: Ruta 40 Km 78, Tunuyán, Mendoza
Call: +54 262-242-4311
Find them on Facebook: YA-CE Lomiteria
Price Range: $

La Posada del Jamon

This hidden gem in Mendoza was created by Don Miguel Cairo and his wife. This unique and traditional restaurant was born under the idea of celebrating pork with tasty dishes. They make their own ham including the speciality *jamon al Malbec* (Malbec ham). They also grow their own vegetables on site and offer delicious local cuisine. With a great wine cellar, this should be on your must-try list.

Address: Ruta 92, Km 13, Vista Flores, Tunuyán, Mendoza
Call: +54 262-249-2053
LaPosadaDelJamon.com.ar

Food Festivals

La Fiesta Nacional del Chivo

In early January in the city of Malargüe, province of Mendoza, is the celebration of *La Fiesta Nacional del Chivo,* the National Goat Festival. This is one of the most important celebrations in the province which draws thousands of chefs and foodies to taste the emblematic Malargüe goat. Hundreds of goats are cooked *a la llama* (over wood flames) during the event. The meat stands out for its gamey herbal flavor and there are many ways of preparing it: stewed, grilled, roasted, and flamed. When you are there, ask for the *chivipan* (goat sausage sandwich).

When: Second or Third week of January for 4 days
Where: Malargüe, Argentina
Information: +54 260-447-0358/447-0396
TurismoMalargue.com/Fiesta-Nacional-del-Chivo-Malargue.html

La Fiesta Nacional de la Vendimia

This 10 day National Harvest Festival and cultural celebration takes place every year in March in the city of Mendoza, attracting thousands of wine lovers from Argentina and beyond. This huge event fills the streets of Mendoza with a carnival atmosphere and is the highlight of the viticulture and winemaking tradition in Argentina. See link to The Welcome **Argentina website** which offers great additional insights on the festival at authenticfoodquest.com/argentinabook.

When: Starts the last Sun of February, between last week of February to first week of March for 10 days
Where: Mendoza, Argentina
Information: +54 261-4495840
Cultura.Mendoza.gov.ar

CAFAYATE

Like the Mendoza region, the Calchaquí Valleys in the province of Salta are famous for the landscape—sweeping rock walls in reds and pinks and oranges—and for the **Torrontés** wine.

With about 12,000 inhabitants, Cafayate sits in the center of this valley on the western slope of the Andes. Situated in the arid river valley 1,683 meters (5,522 ft) above sea level, locals refer to this climate as "the land where the sun lives." A distinct destination of its own, the town is about 189 km (117 mi) from Salta City and 1,329 km (826 mi) from Buenos Aires.

FARMERS MARKETS

Mercado Municipal

There is one permanent farmers market located behind the main plaza of town. You will find a few vendors that open in the morning or later in the day. They have *carnicerías* and *verdulerías* in one store offering a selection of meat, fruit and vegetables.

Address: Pasaje 11 de Noviembre, Cafayate, Salta
Hours: Daily from 8am to 12pm & 4pm to 8pm

FOOD STORES

Local Specialty Stores

You will find many small corner food stores where you can buy food products and household items in town. You will also find stores catering to tourist that sell wines, beers and sweets from the region.

Panificadora Flor Del Valle

This store is conveniently located next to the main plaza. It carries all you need from food to household items. They have a great bakery and a deli section where everything is fresh.

Address: Belgrano 23, Cafayate, Salta
Hours: Mon-Sat, 8am to 1pm & 4pm to 9pm

Heladerias

Dessio

Located on the main square in Cafayate, this artisanal *heladería* sells ice cream made with **Malbec** and **Torrontés** wine. They also offer more traditional Argentine flavors like *dulce de leche*, *sambayon* (made with egg yolks, sugar and white wine) or *tramontana* (made with vanilla and *dulce de leche*). Order the Torrontés flavor as it is definitively a hit.

Address: Vicario Toscano 50, Cafayate, Salta
Hours: Mon-Sat, 8am to 1pm & 4pm to 9pm
Call: +54 386-840-8244
Dessio.net

Helados Miranda

Located a couple blocks north of the main square, this *heladería* is famous in town for having created the wine flavored **helados**. They were closed when we were there without any signs or hours posted, but be sure to stop by and check whether they are open.

Address: Avenida General Güemes Norte 170, Cafayate, Salta
Hours: Tues-Sun, 1:30pm to 12am (check directly at the location)
Call: +54 386-842-1106
Find Helados Miranda on **TripAdvisor.com**

RESTAURANTS

La Casa de las Empanadas

If you want to try or have a craving for *empanadas salteñas*, this is the place to go. With a list of 12 different types of *empanadas*, you can order by the dozen and sample all of them to make a meal out of it. You will also find local specialities such as **locro**, **humitas** and **tamales**. Casual setting with live music a couple of times a week. They have two locations in town.

Address: Mitre 24, Cafayate, Salta
Second location at Nuestra Señora del Rosario 156 Cafayate, Salta
Hours: Tues-Sun from 8pm to 12pm
+54 386-845-4108   **Price Range:** $$
CasaDeLaEmpanada.com.ar

El Hornito

This is a casual restaurant located next to the Mercado Municipal where locals and tourists come together. They offer pizza, *tortas*, **empanadas** and other local dishes at reasonable prices. Look for the massive charcoal oven just outside the entrance of the restaurant. Order beef or chicken *al horno* (from the oven) and pair it with

local wine or beer.
Address: Rivadavia 266, Cafayate, Salta
Hours: Tues to Sun from 8pm to 12pm

Call: +54 386-842-2185
Find them on **TripAdvisor.com**
Price Range: $$

Pacha
Cooking classes offered

This is a hidden gem in Cafayate. Off the beaten path, it is not listed in any guide books, but its Italian flair and fresh-baked delicacies lure the locals. The chef moved from Buenos Aires to Cafayate in search of a less stressful pace of life, and this combined restaurant and tea shop offers cooking classes in addition to homemade bread, fresh pastries and *alfajores*.
Address: Belgrano, 92, Cafayate, Salta
Hours: Wed-Sat from 8pm to 12pm
Lunch by reservation
Call: +54 386-848-0955
Find them on Facebook: Facebook.com/PachaRestauranteCafayate
Price Range: $$$

Restaurant Mercado Municipal

For a truly local and authentic experience, eat at the restaurant inside the **Mercado Municipal**. This basic and unpretentious restaurant sells local specialities like *humitas*, *tamales* and pasta at a very reasonable price.

Address: Pasaje 11 de Noviembre, Cafayate, Salta
Restaurant Hours: Tues-Sun lunch & dinner. Market hours daily from 8am to 12pm & 4pm to 8pm
Price Range: $

You will find more restaurant selections within the wineries.
Check the Wineries of Cafayate section below.

STREET FOOD VENDORS

One block north of the main plaza on Avenida General Güemes Norte is a *tortilla* vendor who offers *jamon y queso* (ham and cheese) or only *queso tortillas*. This vendor is usually here in the afternoon from 3pm until he runs out of *tortillas*.

UNIQUE CULINARY EXPERIENCES

Cooking Classes
Cafayate Immersion Cooking Class

Cafayate Immersion offers original programs that combine local activities like winemaking, biking and hiking tours, as well as pottery and cooking classes.
Where: Calle Colon 253, Cafayate
Email: contact@cafayateimmersion.com
CafayateImmersion.com

Cooking classes are offered at **Pacha Restaurant** and at a few of the **wineries in Cafayate**. Refer to the restaurant section and the section on the wineries of Cafayate below for the contact information.

Wine Museum
Museo de la Vid y del Vino

Before you dive into wine tasting at the *bodegas*, make a detour at the museum dedicated to the wine in Cafayate called Museo de la Vid y del Vino, the "Museum of the Vine and Wine." The first part of the museum does a great job of describing the specificities of the wine region with a touch of poetry. The second part of the museum focuses on the birth of Cafayate as a wine producing region and the early years of production. Wine tasting by the glass is offered at the end of the tour. You can also purchase bottles of wine as well. A great experience that we highly recommend.

Address: Avenida General Güemes Sur esquina Fermín Perdiguero, 4427 Cafayate, Salta
Hours: Tues-Sun, 10am to 7:30pm
Entrance fees: ARS30 for visitors; ARS10 for Argentine nationals & students.
museodelavidyelvino.gov.ar

Winery Tours, Tastings and Cooking Classes

Torrontés

This is Cafayate's emblematic white wine and we sought to understand its mythos by sampling it at various *bodegas*. The wines from Salta are among the highest vineyards in the world with more than 1800 hectares of vines cultivated in the Calchaquí Valleys. Cafayate vines are at 1750 meters above sea level, making them higher than the vines of Mendoza, Burgundy and Bordeaux in France, and Napa Valley in the U.S.

With over 340 sunny days per year, the hot rays of the sun and cool nights produce grapes with a superb ripeness that transmits intense colors and great concentrations of aromas and flavors to the wines.

Unlike Mendoza, Cafayate is a much smaller town and very easy to navigate. There are several *bodegas* to choose from. Some are in town and within walking distance from the city center. Others are within a few kilometers from the city center.

Vasija Secreta   *Restaurant*

Vasija Secreta, the "Secret Vessel" offers free tours and tastings at their *bodega*. The tour starts with the visit of their private museum, then goes on to their production process followed by a free tasting. They also have a great patio to relax and enjoy a glass of wine with **empanadas** or other menu items during lunch hours.

Recommended for its setting and free tastings.
Address: Ruta 40 s/n, 1 km north from downtown Cafayate, Salta
Hours: Mon-Sat, 9:30am to 1pm & 2:30pm to 6pm; Sun from 11am to 1pm & 2:30pm to 6pm. Tours & tastings are free; restaurant open for lunch only.
Call: +54 386-842-1850
VasijaSecreta.com

Bodega Nanni   *Retoño Restaurante*

One of the best tour experiences to have in Cafayate is at Bodega Nanni, which is very conveniently located about one block from the main plaza. Nanni produces organic wines in limited quantities, about 400,000 bottles a year. It is possible to tour their relatively small operation for free without doing a tasting. The tour is followed by a tasting of four of their signature wines including the **Torrontés** and the Tannat, one of the other wines you want to have in Cafayate. They have a lovely garden outside where you can relax while you finish sipping your wine. Nanni is clear about their opening hours and they are one of the vineyards with the most flexible hours. This might be due to the fact that they also run a restaurant inside the *bodega* called Retoño Restaurante.

Address: Silverio Chavarría 151, Cafayate, Salta
Hours: Mon-Sat, 9:30am to 1pm & 2:30pm to 6pm; Sun from 11am to 1pm & 2:30pm to 6pm. Tours are free with ARS30 per person for tasting. Restaurant is open for lunch & dinner.
Call: +54 3868 42-1527
BodegaNanni.com

Bodega Mounier

Known for its organic wines and amazing location at the foot of the mountains, Bodega Mounier is a boutique winery that produces about 50,000 bottles of wines a year. The wines are branded Las Nubes, "the Clouds." They produce the wine organically, although they don't have the organic certification and label.

This familial *bodega* was founded by Jose L. Mounier.
Address: El Divisadero 4427, Cafayate, Argentina
Hours: Mon-Fri 9:30am to 5:30pm; Sat from 9:30am to 2pm. The tour fee of ARS15 per person includes a tasting.
Call: +54 386-842-2129
BodegaMounier.com.ar

Finca Quara

Finca Quara is a large *bodega* on the outskirts of the city on the south side. Free tours and tastings are offered. Try their Tannat Reserva, a nice full-bodied red wine.

Address: Ruta 40 - km 4340, 2 km south of downtown Cafayate, Salta
Hours: Mon to Fri 9:30am to 1pm & 2pm to 4pm; Sat & Sun from 9:30am to 1pm. Tours & tastings are free.
Call: +54 386-842-1709   FincaQuara.com

El Porvenir
Restaurant - Cooking classes offered

This *bodega* is housed in a renovated building with preserved adobe walls, a few blocks north of the main square. In addition to tours and tastings, they also offer lunch and cooking lessons to learn how to make *empanadas*!

Address: Cordoba 32, Cafayate, Salta
Hours: Tues-Sat, 9am to 1pm & 3pm to 6pm; Sun & Mon from 9am to 1pm. Tours are free; tasting is ARS60 per person.
Call: +54 386-842-2007
ElPorvenirDeCafayate.com/en

Salvador Figueroa

This is a really small family run winery located in the center of town. Only 13,000 bottles of Torrontés and Malbec are produced each year. There is no tour offered and you can get a simple tasting (2 wines) for a very reasonable fee. It is worth visiting in between *bodegas* or while waiting for the next tour to start at Nanni or El Porvenir.

Address: 20 de Junio 25, Cafayate, Salta
Hours: Mon-Sat, 9:30am to 12:30pm & 3pm to 7pm, Sun from 10:30am to 12:30pm Tastings are ARS10 per person.
Call: +54 3868-842-1125
CavaCafayate.com.ar/Salvador_Figueroa.htm

El Transito

This *bodega* is located between Nanni and Salvador Figueroa *bodegas*. The tour experience at this winery was rushed and the guide was not comfortable answering questions, but you might have a different experience.

Address: Belgrano 102, Cafayate, Argentina.
Hours: Mon to Sat from 9am to 1pm & 3pm to 7pm; Sun from 10am to 2pm & 3pm to 6pm. Tastings are ARS20 per person.
Call: +54 387-431-7429
BodegaElTransito.com

El Esteco
Restaurant

This is the second largest *bodega* in Cafayate, with tours and tastings and a restaurant for lunch. They are closed in the afternoons on the weekends.

Address: Ruta 40 y Ruta 68, Cafayate, Salta
Hours: Mon-Fri, 10am to 12pm & 2:30pm to 6:30pm; Sat & Sun from 10am to 12pm
Call: +54 386-842-1139 / 115-198-8000
elEsteco.com

Etchart

At the time of this writing, the winery was closed to tourists for renovation, but they have a store across from the *bodega* where you can buy their quality wines. It is located about 2 km south of Cafayate.
Address: Ruta Nacional N° 40, Km 4338, Cafayate, Argentina.
Call: +54 386-842-1310 / 1312
BodegasEtchart.com

Domingo Hermanos

This is a family *bodega* and the largest in Cafayate with more than 90 hectares of grape vineyards, mainly **Torrontés**, **Malbec** and Cabernet Sauvignon. Their location is really close to the main square, about three blocks south. They offer tours and tastings in a nice garden setting. You can also visit their goat farm, **Cabras de Cafayate**.
Address: Nuestra Señora del Rosario s/n, Cafayate, Salta
Hours: Mon-Fri, 9am-12:30pm & 3pm to 7pm; Sat & Sun from 9am to 12:30pm
Call: +54 386-842-1225
DomingoHermanos.com

Piattelli Vineyards *Restaurant*

This *bodega* is owned by a visionary Minnesota native passionate about Argentina's wine. It is located on the north side of Cafayate, housed in a modern building where you can enjoy lunch on the terrace with views of the beautiful Calchaquí Valley. They offer tours and tastings.
Address: Camino a Yacochuya, Cafayate, Salta
Hours: Daily from 9:30am to 6pm. Tours & tastings are ARS80 per person.
Call: +54 386-841-8214
PiattelliVineyards.com

---

6 TIPS TO MAKE THE MOST OF YOUR WINERY VISIT IN CAFAYATE

1. Visit the **Museo de la Vid y del Vino** to grasp what make Cafayate wines so special.
2. You can drop into most wineries; reservations are not necessary unless you plan to eat at the winery restaurant.
3. Have plenty of Argentine pesos handy as very few wineries accept credit cards.
4. Visits and wine tastings tend to be under one hour. Combined with the fact that several wineries are within walking distance. It is possible to visit more than four wineries in one day. Keep in mind that the last tour is usually one hour before closing.
5. Plan your visit during the week; over the weekend, Cafayate slows down quite a bit and not many wineries are open. Check hours with individual wineries before your visit; the hours posted at the tourist office and online are not always accurate.
6. Hire remis (taxis) to get to some of the furthest wineries from town. You can find very reasonably priced rides, but you should agree on the price before your ride.

Winery Outside of Cafayate
Colomé

Founded in 1831, this secluded *bodega* is one of the oldest wineries in Argentina, owned by a wealthy Swiss family with a unique social approach to the business that includes the local community. They brought biodynamic practices to the winery, which is home to some of the world's highest vineyards at 2,300 to 3,111 meters above sea level (7,500-10,000 ft). Nested in this beautiful setting, you will find an art museum on site. If your travels and your budget allow, you can stay at the hotel and enjoy their restaurant. Colomé is located about 3 hours north of Cafayate in the Upper Calchaquí Valleys, 20 km (12 mi) from Molinos.

Address: Ruta Prov. 52, Km 20, Molinos 4419, Salta
Hours: Daily from 9:30am to 6pm. Museum closed Mons & mornings. Tour & tasting ARS50 per person; reservations required.
Call: +54-386-849-4200
BodegaColome.com

Farm Tour
Cabras de Cafayate

Goat cheese is one of the typical products from the Northwest part of Argentina. Cabras de Cafayate, located about 3 km (1.5 mi) from Cafayate, is a unique goat farm that revolutionized cheese production and sanitary control. This unique goat farm is part of **Domingo Hermanos** winery, one of the most renowned wineries of Cafayate. After a tour of the goat farm and cheese production, sample their delicious cheese. To read more about our experience visiting this goat farm, see the "**Touring a Goat Farm in a Winery**" at authenticfoodquest.com/argentinabook.

Address: Finca Auletta fracción G y H, Cafayate, Salta
Hours: Mon-Fri, 9am to 1pm & 3pm to 6pm; Sat & Sun from 9am to 1pm. Tour & goat cheese tasting is ARS10, & takes one hour. Check directly with the farm as their hours are subject to change.
Call: +54 386-842-2050
CabrasDeCafayate.todowebsalta.com.ar

Food Festivals
Fiesta Nacional Del Vino Torrontés

This is Argentina's most famous white wine festival, devoted to Torrontés. It is celebrated in November, when the Torrontés grapes reach maturity. Full of festivities, you will find lots of wine, traditional folk music, revelry and food. You are in Salta Province, so expect *empanadas salteñas* to feature prominently.

When: Second half of November
Where: Cafayate
Call: +54-387-431-0950
Email: muncafayate@hotmail.com
FiestasNacionales.org/fiesta/327/Fiesta_Nacional_del_Vino_Torrontes

Semana del Torrontés

Celebrated in October, this "Week of Torrontés" includes themed tastings at the different local *bodegas*. There are music shows as well as tastings of local food specialities.

When: Second week of October
Where: Cafayate
Call: +54-387-431-0950
SemanaDelTorrontes.com.ar

The Andean Northwest Region

SALTA

Nicknamed *Salta La Linda* (Salta the Beautiful), this charming Spanish colonial town was founded in 1582 by Spanish commander Hernando de Lerma. Today, Salta is emerging as a popular tourist destination filled with local food specialities and amazing architecture.

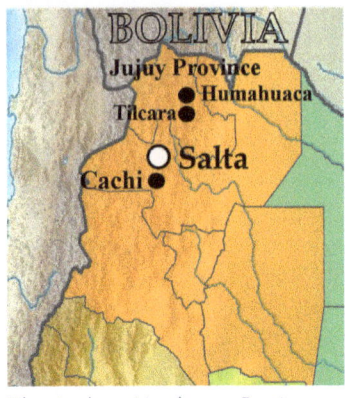

The Andean Northwest Region - Based on B1mbo work

FARMERS MARKETS

Mercado Municipal San Miguel

This market, located four blocks from the main square, is housed in a historical monument of the city of Salta. With an area of approximately 10,000 square meters, it has four main entrances, one on each of the surrounding streets: Avenida San Martin, Urquiza, La Florida and Ituzaingó. You will find many type of vendors including, vegetables, fruits, meat, spices and other household utilities. This market feels more like a bazaar than a market. You will find regional specialities on the second level.

Address: General Urquiza 781, Salta
Hours: Mon-Sat, 8am to 1:30pm & 5pm to 9:30pm
Find them on: Viajeros.com

Mercadito Belgrano

You will find this local market situated on the north side of the city. There are eight main sections with vendors selling poultry, fish, fruits and vegetables, meat, pasta and *empanadas*.

Address: Vicente Lopez & 12 de Octubre, Salta.
Hours: Mon-Sat, 8am to 1pm & from 5pm to 9pm

FOOD STORES

The Big Stores

Vea

This is the main supermarket in Salta. You will find all the products you need including dairy, produce, fruits and vegetables, but not many local options.

Address: Florida 50, Salta
Hours: Mon-Fri, 8am to 10:30pm; Sat from 8am to 10pm; Sun from 9am to 9pm
SupermercadosVea.com.ar

Other supermarkets include Dia (**SupermercadosDia.com.ar**) which are lower end supermarkets. You will also find local convenience stores which will be your best alternative for fruits and vegetables in addition to the market.

Local Specialty Stores

Heladeria

Rosmari

This is one of the best local artisanal ice cream stores in Salta. This is a classic stop for local Salteña families and a place you should not miss on your travels. Choose from several varieties of **dulce de leche** and chocolate. Make this your preferred stop to take a break from the heat.

Address: Pueyrredón 202, Salta
RosmariArtesanal.com.ar

Rotisserie

Chiquilin Pollo a la Parrilla

This corner take-away rotisserie offers fully cooked chicken or chicken pieces to go with fresh homemade fries. The chicken is cooked on a *parrilla* visible from the outside of the store. A great delight for an easy meal to go. They also sell chorizo, sausages and grilled pork belly.

Address: Avenida Belgrano 295, Salta
Call: +54 387-421-1408

RESTAURANTS

El Charrua

This two-floor *parrilla* restaurant attracts locals and tourists alike. They grill different cuts of beef and other meats on the *parrilla*, and they also have a few local seasonal specialities. Their portions are not small; you might want to share. They have a second, more casual location on Caseros Street.

Address: General Güemes 186, Salta
Second location on Caseros 221, Salta
Hours: Open daily at 12pm
Call: +54 387-422-5166 / 432-2222
ParrillaelCharrua.com.ar
Price Range: $$

La Tacita

This corner cafe makes arguably the best *empanadas* in Salta. They prepare the *empanadas* fresh on site and bake them in their clay oven per order, so be prepared to wait with a nice local *salteña* beer. The *empanadas* are served really hot, so let them cool down and enjoy with the red salsa that accompanies them. They have just a few types of *empanadas* so make sure you try them all!

Address: Caseros 396, Salta
Hours: Mon-Sat, 8am to 12am; Sun from 10am to 3pm
Call: +54 387-431-8289
Find them on: Viajeros.com
Price Range: $

El Patio de la Empanada

This is an open-air restaurant with about 5-7 vendors competing for your business. As soon as you walk in, menus will be thrust at you and people will usher to sit you in their respective areas. Despite the welcome, pick a table wherever you feel like it. Menus include many different types of *empanadas*, *tamales*, and *humitas*, all made on the spot and delicious. Try the *empanadas de arabes* (prepared with beef) and *empanadas de charqui* (llama jerky).

Address: Avenida San Martin esquina Esteco, Salta
Hours: Mon to Sun from 7am to 12am
Call: +54 387-431-4484
Find them on: Viajeros.com
Price Range: $

Jovi Dos

This large casual restaurant is located on a corner of Balcarce Street across Plaza Güemes. It is a lively area at night where the *peñas* (local bars) play folk music. This restaurant has plenty of seatings indoors and outdoors. They have casual cuisine with some local specialities like *empanadas*, *humitas*, and *tamales*.

Address: Balcarce 601, Salta
Hours: Daily from 12pm to 3pm & 8pm to 2am
Call: +54 387-432-9438
Find them on: TripAdvisor.com
Price Range: $$

La Casona del Molino

This restaurant was recommended to us by one of the instructors at the local School of Gastronomy. It is located on the west side of town, with regional cuisine and folk music.

Address: Luis Burela 1, Salta
Hours: Tues-Sun from 12pm to 3:30pm & 9pm to 3:30am
Call: +54 387-434-2835
Find them on Facebook: Facebook.com/LaCasonaDelMolino
Price Range: $$

Chirimoya

This cute vegetarian restaurant is located three blocks east of the main square. With local dishes like *humitas* made with soy meat, they offer nice meat alternatives, with food to go or for delivery.

Address: España 211, Salta, Argentina
Hours: Mon-Fri, 9:30am to 3am; Sat from 10am to 3pm
Call: +54 387-431-2857
Find them on Facebook: Facebook.com/Chirimoya.Vegetariano
Price Range: $$

UNIQUE CULINARY ACTIVITIES

Food Festival

Fiesta Nacional del Tamal

The National Tamal Festival is part folk festival—celebrating the *gaucho* culture with dressage, music, and dance—and part food festival, with local specialities that include of course, the most delicious *tamales* as well as *locro*, *humita*, *empanadas salteñas* and *asado*. This three-day event takes place during the second half of July each year in Chicoana, located about one hour south of Salta.

When: Three days in the second half of July
Where: Chicoana
Call: +54 387-490-7019
FiestasNacionales.org/fiesta/323/Fiesta_Nacional_del_Tamal

Fiesta Nacional de la Empanada

The National Empanada Festival takes place in Tucuman, a city known for its delicious *empanadas*, located four hours southeast of Salta. This festival, which last for three days in mid-September, is essentially a gastronomic event that combines the celebration for the best *empanadas* with folk music and dance performances. You will try all sorts of *empanadas* with a variant from each region cooked in the clay oven used for the festival. The National Empanada Festival, now in its thirty-fifth edition, culminates with the election of the National Champion of Empanada.

When: Three days in mid-September
Where: San Miguel de Tucuman
Call: +54 387-490-7019
Email: informes@tucumanturismo.gov.ar
FiestasNacionales.org/fiesta/252/Fiesta_Nacional_de_la_Empanada

CACHI

Cachi is a charming village with adobe houses, paved streets and Spanish Colonial architecture. It is situated at 2,280m above sea level in the Alto Calchaquí Valley, about three hours west from Salta. Most of its 5,500 inhabitants are descendants of the Diaguita-Calchaquí culture which also has influences from the Incas. The "Valle Encantado" (Enchanted Valley) and Los Cardones National Park make Cachi a popular destination.

The land is mostly arid but fertile enough to grow vegetables and legumes, especially peppers. If you happen to visit Cachi, take a moment to appreciate the local cuisine at the local cafés and restaurants.

RESTAURANTS

Nevado de Cachi

This restaurant offers local specialities such as *locro* and *cabrito* in a nice casual setting. Here, you can try their *empanadas de quinoa*.

Address: Colonel R. Llanos y F. Suárez, Cachi, Salta
Hours: Mon-Fri, 12am to 5pm & 9pm to 3am
Call: +54 386-849-0080
RestaurantNevadoDeCachi.com
Price Range: $$

Restaurant Catalino

This restaurant was recommended to us by a local resident. It is located in the hotel El Cortijo, a few blocks southwest of the main square. They offer delicious local specialities with a touch of creativity at very reasonable prices.

Address: Avenida del Automóvil Club Argentino s/n, El Cortijo Hotel, Cachi
Call: +54 386-849-1054
elCortijoHotel.com
Price Range: $$

UNIQUE CULINARY ACTIVITIES

Food Festival

Fiesta Nacional del Pimiento

This National Chili Pepper Festival takes place in Payogasta, located 15 minutes north of Cachi, during the second half of July. This event combines tradition, folklore and cuisine celebrating the work of the farmers who devote their efforts to the farming of chili peppers. The chili pepper is used for the production of paprika, and is traditionally dried on the slopes of the hills. The drying peppers create a beautiful red blanket on the hills, adding to the stunning landscape of the Calchaquí Valley. The production of pepper for paprika is an important economic activity throughout the region of Valles Calchaquíes, and therefore merits a celebration. Tasting of regional dishes, folkloric shows and popular dances are some of the main attractions of this more than 40-years-old festival.

When: Second half of October
Where: Payogasta
Information: +54-386-849-6033
FiestasNacionales.org/fiesta/316/Fiesta_Nacional_del_Pimiento

JUJUY PROVINCE - Quebrada de Humahuaca

The Quebrada de Humahuaca is a UNESCO Heritage gorge in a narrow mountain valley known for its beautiful landscape made of rock formations that reveal waves of colors. Located north of Jujuy the capital of the Jujuy province, the Quebrada is also unique for its indigenous communities that are perpetuating the Andean tradition, culture and local meals in the region.

HUMAHUACA

Humahuaca is the principal and largest town of the Quebrada de Humahuaca, recognizable by the large *Monumento de la Independencia* dominating the city. At its top, you will have a nice view of the Valley and the river (Rio Grande) as well as the city. The Argentina border with Bolivia is only about 160 km (100 mi) away.

FARMERS MARKETS

Mercado Municipal de Humahuaca

In the tourist part of town, you will find a small food market located two blocks from the main square. Here, you find vegetables, fruits and meat vendors. You can also find *empanadas* and juices to go.

Address: Avenida Belgrano y esquina Tucuman, Humahuaca, Jujuy
Hours: Daily from 9am to 1pm & 4pm to 8pm

RESTAURANTS

Aisito Resto Bar

This restaurant might be victim of its own success, having appeared in a tourist guide book. The prices are slightly inflated, though it remains a solid option with nice regional dishes. Try the *salad de quinoa*, a refreshing option. They have wifi and you can pay by credit card.

Address: Buenos Aires 435, Humahuaca, Jujuy
Hours: Daily from 11am to 3pm & 7pm to 12am
Call: +54 388-488-6609 / 431-2945
Find them on Facebook: Facebook.com/AisitoEspacioCultural
Price Range: $$

Los Patios de Lucia

This is a nice hidden gem in Humahuaca. This couple owned restaurant makes homemade regional cuisine and local specialities. You will find fresh salads, *tamales*, *humitas* and *locro* at very reasonable prices. They have a nice garden where they grow some of their produce. Enjoy your meal on their nice outdoor patio!

Address: Cordoba 89, Humahuaca, Jujuy
Information: +54 388-523-9239 / 531-6946
Find them on Facebook: Facebook.com/Los-patios-de-Lucia-433806356763595
Price Range: $

TILCARA

San Francisco de Tilcara (its full name) is located 45 km south of Humahuaca in the province of Jujuy. With a population of almost six thousand inhabitants, the city sits at 2461 m (8,074 ft) in the middle of the Quebrada de Humahuaca. With many lodging and accommodation options, It is usually the base town chosen by travelers to explore the valley.

FARMERS MARKET

Mercado Municipal

Located in the lower part of town, this market is your best option for your groceries. In the covered part of the market, you will find vendors selling vegetables, fruits, cheese and meat. In the outdoor area of the market, in addition of the fruit and vegetables vendors, you will find vendors selling native grains such as corn, **quinoa** and more. There are also a few food vendors selling *empanadas*, pizzas and locally prepared dishes.

Address: Bolivar 244, Tilcara, Jujuy
Hours: Daily from 9am to 1pm & 4pm to 9pm

RESTAURANTS

Khuska

This restaurant located on the upper side of town stands out from the many restaurants catering to tourists in the center of town. Chef Inés prepares exquisite local meals with a touch of creativity. Order the *sopa de quinoa* to start. Indulge in the *cazuela de llama* for the main meal. If you still have room, try the local desert *cayote con quesillo y nuez*.

Address: Dr. Ernesto Padilla 581, Tilcara, Jujuy
Hours: Tues-Sat, 7:30pm to 12pm
Call: +54 388-478-7356
Find them on: TripAdvisor.com
Price Range: $$

La Peña de Carlitos

For music and a cultural experience, one of the best options is La Peña de Carlitos located downtown Tilcara. The restaurant offers regional cuisine and live traditional music every night. Reservations are recommended for dinner on the weekends. Try their *empanadas de quinoa* and *empanadas de llama*!

Address: Lavalle 397 esq. Rivadavia, Tilcara, Jujuy
Hours: Daily from 10am to 2am
Information: +54 155-483-7278
Find them on: TripAdvisor.com
Price Range: $$

Quebrada Querida

This restaurant is located next to the bus terminal. This is a new option in town that proposes homemade cuisine at reasonable prices. They also have vegan and vegetarian items. A nice change from the touristy restaurants!

Address: Belgrano 688, Casi esquina Alverro, Tilcara
Hours: Daily from 5pm to 1am
Call: +54 112-332-5113
Find them on Facebook: Facebook.com/QuebradaQueridaDeTilcara
Price Range: $

STREET FOOD VENDORS

You will find a few vendors of *tortillas*, mainly next to the bus station in the lower part of town. Shop around, check the food, ask the price and make your choice!

UNIQUE CULINARY ACTIVITIES

Food Festivals

Festival del Queso y La Cabra

If you find yourself in January in the Quebrada de Humahuaca, don't miss out on the Cheese and Goat Festival. The *cabra* (goat) is found in the high altitude of the Quebrada de Humahuaca. Goats are used for their milk and when it comes to food, *queso de cabra* (goat cheese) is incredibly popular. At the festival you will be able to taste various types of *queso de cabra*. Try it with *pan casero*, the local flat bread.

When: Second or third week in January
Where: Chorrillos 8 km north of Humahuaca, Jujuy
Call: +54 388-742-1375
elTribuno.info/
xv-Festival-del-Queso-y-la-Cabra-n664042

Patagonia & the Lake Region

Patagonia is a vast and sparsely populated region crossed by the southern section of the Andes as well as deserts, steppes and grasslands. Encompassing most of the bottom cone of South America, it is shared by both Argentina and Chile.

BARILOCHE

Bariloche, also known as San Carlos de Bariloche, is one of the most attractive cities in Argentina and a popular holiday and outdoor destination. It is located on the southwest part of the country close to the Chilean border. Situated on the shores of Nahuel Huapi Lake and the foothills of the Andes, it is a beautiful city with spectacular views and exquisite scenery.

Patagonia & the Lake Region - Based on B1mbo work

Bariloche sells itself as "Little Switzerland" based on the weather, architecture, chocolates and abundance of Saint Bernard dogs. The Swiss construction style uses Patagonian hardwood and stone, adopted from Switzerland. In addition to the Swiss architecture, there is a grander draw that brings tourists to Bariloche: the **chocolate**. A surprisingly large number of chocolatiers are concentrated on Mitre Avenue, or what Argentines call "The Avenue of Chocolate Dreams."

Patagonia is home to Argentina's best lamb and wild game, deer, and wild rabbits. European immigrants who moved to Bariloche in the early 20th century brought their traditions, customs and foods with them, including fondue and charcuterie, which now uses native meats. The meat specialities in Bariloche include: *ciervo* (deer) and *jabali* (wild boar) as well as *cordero* Patagonico (Patagonian lamb).

Bariloche is surrounded by mountains, rivers, forests, lakes and dominated by the Andean mountain range. It is an exceptionally beautiful city offering numerous summer and winter outdoor activities. Fishing, including fly fishing for *trucha*, trout, is a popular sport in the several lakes and rivers in the region. Finally, Bariloche is also known for its production of local artisanal craft beers for more than 100 years.

FARMERS MARKET

Mercado Comunitario Municipal

Bariloche is starting to develop its farmers markets. This market is located far from the city center in a local neighborhood. Situated on a side street with no signage, it is difficult to find and rather small. Closed at the time of our visit, the local people didn't seem to know much about it. At this time, we are not sure it is worth the effort to come here unless you are motorized. If you are downtown, it is best to stick with the *verdulería* and other speciality stores that are located in the center of town.

Address: Santa Cruz 1120, San Carlos de Bariloche
Hours: Tues-Fri, 9am to 1pm & 3pm to 7pm; Sat 9am to 1pm
Find them on Facebook: Facebook.com/MunicipalidadDeBariloche/videos/915896578456259/

FOOD STORES

The Big Stores

La Anonima

The most popular food store in Bariloche. The address below is the closest location to downtown.

Address: Quaglia 311/333, San Carlos de Bariloche
Hours: Mon-Sat, 9am to 9:30pm; Sun from 10am to 1:30pm & 5pm to 9pm
LaAnonima.com.ar

Supermercado Todo

Located on the east side of town, this supermarket is well stocked for all your needs. There is limited availability of regional products.

Address: Vice Almte O'Connor 824, San Carlos de Bariloche
Hours: Mon-Sat, 9am to 7pm
STodo.com.ar

Local Specialty Stores

Panaderías

Lo Integral

Lo Integral is one of the best bakeries in Argentina! It is one of the few that makes only whole wheat or *integral* products including **alfajores** and **medialunas**. They also offer vegetarian sandwiches, fresh pasta, and vegan products. They have delicious bread and cookies. A rare find in Argentina.

Address: Vice O'Connor 650, San Carlos de Bariloche
Hours: Mon-Sat from 8am to 8:30pm

Panadería Trevisan

This is a traditional bakery that offers a very nice selection of bread, sweets and sandwiches made fresh for the day. They have five locations in town. Check their website for the one most conveniently located to you.

Address: 12 de Octubre y Es&i, San Carlos de Bariloche (east side of town)
Second location at Moreno 76, San Carlos de Bariloche (downtown location)
PanaderiaTrevisan.com.ar

Verdulerías

When it comes to *verdulerias*, you might want to avoid the overpriced stores in the downtown area. Instead, visit the local stores a few blocks from the center.

Verdulería y Frutería "La Papa"

Small fruit and vegetables store; you will find tasty produces for most of your need.

Address: Morales 510, San Carlos de Bariloche.
Hours: Daily from 9am to 10pm
Find them on Facebook: Facebook.com/FrutiVerdulaPapa/info?tab=overview

Verdulería R y K

This small *verdulería* is located in the direction of the bus station. They offer a limited selection of fruits and vegetables for a very reasonable price. They also sell fresh eggs.

Address: Corner of 12 de Octubre y Namuncura, San Carlos de Bariloche, Argentina

Pasta Stores

Piú Pasta

They make a range of fresh pasta every day, including salmon and lamb **ravioles**. The pastas here are arguably some of the best we had in Argentina.

Address: Belgrano 126, San Carlos de Bariloche
Hours: Mon-Sat from 9am to 2pm & 5pm to 9:30pm; Sun 9:30am to 2pm
Call: +54 294-442-2408
Find them on Facebook: Facebook.com/PiuPasta

Deli & Rotisserie

La Casanova

This store offers prepared meals, deli meat, prepared food and chicken to go. You can find ciervo the local wild meat speciality here.

Address: 12 de Octubre 1569, San Carlos de Bariloche
Call: +54 294-440-0253

Cheese and Cured Meats Stores

La Pata Negra

In Bariloche, you would think it would be easy to find cured meat and cheese stores. But beyond the touristy store from the Family Weiss, it is not easy to find a good deli store. Fortunately there is La Pata Negra, a regional cheese and cured meat store that provides great quality products. We definitively recommend visiting this store to prepare your picnic if you're planning on hiking in the region.

Address: Belgrano 126, San Carlos de Bariloche, Argentina
Hours: Mon-Sat, 8:30am to 1:30pm & 5:30pm to 9:30pm
LaPataNegra.com.ar

Heladeria

Jauja

This might be the best artisanal ice creams from Argentina. Originally from El Bolson, a city two hours south of Bariloche, it has grown to many locations in Patagonia and now in Buenos Aires due to its popularity. Don't miss their chocolate ice cream in the capital of Chocolate!

Address: Moreno 48, San Carlos de Bariloche
Hours: Mon-Fri, 9am to 11:30pm; Sat 9:30am to 1am; Sun 10:30am to 11:30pm
Call: +54-294-443-7888
Jauja.com.ar

Seafood Stores

Delicias del Mar

There are several pescaderia in Bariloche, but one large pescaderia to visit is **Delicias del Mar**. They offer trout, prepared seafood dishes and even pasta for sale. A great place to get your fish intake.

Address: Elordi y Vice Almirante O'Connor 0294, San Carlos de Bariloche
Hours: Mon-Sat, 10am to 2pm & 4pm to 9pm; Sun from 11am to 2pm
Find them on Facebook: Facebook.com/Delicias-del-Mar-en-Bariloche-1109664759047757

Chocolate Stores

Mamushka

One of the most striking features of this store is the huge *matryoshka* nesting dolls (Russian dolls) displayed at the entrance and throughout the store. This store dominates a prime corner of the street and is a busy and popular stop. It serves high quality chocolate. Taste the milk chocolate balls that look like "Ferrero Rocher" chocolates. Mamushka is said to make the best chocolate in Bariloche.

Address: Mitre 298, San Carlos de Bariloche
Hours: Daily from 9:15am to 10pm.
Mamuschka.com

Abuela Goye

Abuela Goye is conveniently located in between **Mamushka** and **Rapa Nui**. It is one of the long-time chocolatiers in Bariloche. They take a homemade and artisanal approach, using ingredients from Patagonia with a focus on sustainability and on minimizing the environmental impact of their products. Taste their full size samples of milk chocolate with *dulce de leche*. And take the opportunity to sample their chocolate *helados* (ice cream). A nice stop on the Avenida del Chocolate.

Address: Mitre 298, San Carlos de Bariloche
Hours: Daily from 9:15am to 10pm
AbuelaGoye.com

Rapa Nui

You can't miss Rapa Nui on Avenida Mitre with its large storefront and its beautiful chocolate fountain. Rapa Nui started as a family owned business by Diego Fenoglio, the son of the pioneer of chocolate in Bariloche, Alfredo Fenoglio. It is a large store which also sells ice cream and tea. Sample the milk chocolate with creamy peanut paste. Worth checking out.

Address: Mitre 202, San Carlos de Bariloche, Argentina
Hours: Mon- Fri, 8am to 10:30pm; Sat & Sun 9am to 10:30pm
ChocolatesRapaNui.com.ar

Torres

Walking into Torres is like walking into an artisanal family owned store. The stores (three in Bariloche) are smaller, more intimate, and offer a much more personalized experience. Here you will have a chance not only to sample the chocolates, but also to learn how they make chocolates by hand: nothing is left to machines and each part of the process is tenderly handled. Try the dark chocolate; it is creamy and soft.

Address: Mitre 222, San Carlos de Bariloche
Hours: Mon-Sat, 9am to 8pm
Information: ChocolatesTorres.com

Chocolate Patagonico

Chocolate Patagonico has a smaller store on the Avenue of Chocolate Dreams. They offer chocolate samples such as milk chocolate with a milk cream chocolate paste in the middle. A nice change from the large bustling stores. Definitively worth a visit!

Address: Mitre 28, San Carlos de Bariloche
Hours: Mon-Sat, 9am to 8pm
ChocolatesPatagonicos.com

Chocolates del Turista

There are several large and imposing Chocolates del Turista stores in Bariloche (franchise owned). They have been around for over 50 years. Their focus is on tourists and visitors with different souvenir packages prepared for sale. Their store on Avenida St. Martin has a production making process that is open for the public to visit. You can see the creamy and delicious chocolate in the making. This alone is worth visiting.

Address: Avenida San Martín 252, San Carlos de Bariloche
Hours: Daily from 9am to 8pm
DelTuristaChocolates.com

RESTAURANTS

Alto El Fuego

At Alto El Fuego, the chef Mathias specialized in meals made on the *parrilla*. Walking into Alto El Fuego is like walking into a little rustic and cozy dining room. On the simple menu, you will find beef, lamb and trout all cooked on the *parrilla*. The serving sizes at Alto El Fuego Parrilla are large enough to share. Order the **Patagonian lamb** or the *trucha* to delight your tastebuds!

Address: 20 de Febrero 451, San Carlos de Bariloche
Hours: Mon-Sat, 12pm to 3pm & 8pm to 12am
Call: +54 294-443-7015
AltoelFuego.com.ar
Price Range: $$

La Salamandra Pulpería

Recommended by Mathias, the chef at Alto Fuego, this cozy restaurant offers a limited menu with delicacies like *empanadas*, *choripán* and steak. The owners offer a friendly and personable service. It is located six kilometers from the center of Bariloche on the Llao Llao route.

Address: Avenida Exequiel Bustillo 5818, San Carlos de Bariloche
Hours: Wed-Sun from 7:30pm to 10:30pm
Call: +54 294-444-1568
Find them on: TripAdvisor.com
Price Range: $$

La Fonda Tio

This is a family style restaurant also recommended to us by locals. It is located in the east side of town. They serve nice portions of local and classic Argentine staples. Good food at reasonable prices.

Address: Bartolome Mitre 1140, San Carlos de Bariloche
Hours: Mon-Sat, 12pm to 3:30pm & 8pm to 12am
Call: +54 294 443-5011
LaFondaDelTio.com.ar
Price Range: $

Ahumadero Weiss

Familia Weiss is known for introducing smoked fish, meats and cheese in Bariloche. They offer an interesting menu based on the smoked products they produce. They also have the speciality lamb *empanadas* for a reasonable price.

Address: Valte O'Connor 401, San Carlos de Bariloche, Argentina
Hours: Daily from 12pm to 4pm & 8pm to 12am
Call: +54 294-443-5874
AhumaderoWeiss.com
Price Range: $$

Cassis

This unique restaurant outside of Bariloche offers gourmet meals prepared with fresh and local products. The restaurant is located on the shore of the Lago Gutiérrez, about 20 minutes from Bariloche center.

Address: Ruta 82 Km. 5,5, San Carlos de Bariloche, Argentina
Hours: Mon-Sat, 9pm to 11pm. Reservations highly recommended. Hours vary depending of the season.
Call: +54 294-447-6167
Cassis.com.ar
Price Range: $$$

STREET FOOD VENDORS

There is a popular **food stand** located near one of the busiest bus stops in the center of town. It is on Avenida San Martin, at the crossing with Morales. You will see locals lining up to pick up their *choripán*. It is a great location to grab a sandwich on the go while waiting for the local buses to visit the region.

UNIQUE CULINARY ACTIVITIES

Chocolate Museum
Museo del Chocolate

The Museum of Chocolate is located a short walk away from the main plaza in the city. This small museum provides a rich history of cocoa, chocolate, and how chocolate came to Bariloche. Guided visits are provided, with one tour in English per day. You will get free samples and hot chocolate with your entrance fee. If you want to linger, there is a little restaurant and store where you can order more chocolate.

Address: Avenida Bustillo 1200, San Carlos de Bariloche
Hours: Daily from 10am to 8pm, ARS20
Call: +54 294-442-2170
Email: guiasdelmuseo@gmail.com
MuseoChocolate.com.ar

Food Festivals
La Fiesta Nacional del Chocolate

Bariloche lives up to its name "Little Switzerland" with its chocolate heritage. Chocoholics unite in Bariloche for the National Chocolate Festival every Easter, where a giant Easter egg more than 8 meters (26 ft) high is broken and shared with thousands of attendees. Chocolate making, music, and cultural events make this a popular and well attended event.

When: Easter week (March/April)
Where: San Carlos de Bariloche
Call: +54 294-442-9850
BarilocheTurismo.gob.ar/actividades/La-Fiesta-del-Chocolate

La Semana de La Cerveza Artesanal

The Week of Artisanal Beer is the largest event for craft beer in Patagonia. Featuring more than 50 craft brew styles, 16 breweries are represented. There is also an important gastronomic fair during the festival in addition to live music and rock bands.

When: First week of December
Where: San Carlos de Bariloche
BeerArt.com.ar

Fiesta Nacional del Asado

The National Asado Festival lasts three days and takes place in the first half of February in Cholila in the province of Chubut. Cholila is a village located about three hours (by car) south of Bariloche. "Cholila" in the indigenous Mapuche language means "beautiful valley," and this festival takes place at the intersection of four splendid valleys: the valley "El Cajon", the valley "El Rincón", the valley "El Blanco" and the valley "Villa Lago Rivadavia." The festival celebrates the *gaucho* culture and the gastronomy events have center stage. You will see the installation of more than 150 roasters. There are more than twenty chefs handling the fire to roast about 10,000 kilos of beef, 400 sausages and 300 lambs!

When: First week of February
Where: Predio el Morro, Cholila (province of Chubut)
Call: +54 294-549-8202
Email: info@turismocholila.gov.ar
TurismoRuta40.com.ar/Cholila.html#

COLONIA SUIZA

When the Goye brothers came across this landscape in 1895, it reminded them of Switzerland. They had traveled through Chile and Valais in French Switzerland, but settled here, 25 km west of Bariloche in a small village now known as Colonia Suiza.

The main activity in Colonia Suiza is tourism. Here you will find excellent cuisine, craft beer, pastries and tea houses, smoked products and regional jams. The tea houses offer some local delicacies such as farm fruits and vegetables, strudel and cakes with berries, natural raspberries and goat cheeses.

UNIQUE CULINARY EXPERIENCES

Brewery Visit

Berlina

Set in nature, at the edge of Colonia Suiza, you will find this craft brewery that is taking over the Argentine craft beer market. They offer a tour of their beer production. You can sample several beers that they brew on site. It is a nice tour to do on your visit in Colonia Suiza.

Address: S.A. Ruta 79 & F. Goye, Colonia Suiza, San Carlos de Bariloche
Call: +54 294-445-4393
CervezaBerlina.com

Curanto

Curanto at Restaurante Victor Goye

The *curanto* introduced by the Goye brothers is the main attraction at *Colonia Suiza*. It is a way of cooking in a pit, underground, using hot stones and leaves to cover food. Check the *curanto* description in the Savor This section for more on this local delicacy. Every Wednesday and Sunday the Curanto is made for locals and tourists alike. Reserve your spot ahead of time on their website.. They cook about 250 portions that day, and it is a popular feast.

Address: Colonia Suiza, San Carlos de Bariloche
Hours: Wed & Sun from 10am to 5pm
Call: +54 294-444-8605
CurantoVictorGoye.com.ar/Bariloche

Trout Farms

Criadero Truchas Colonia Suiza   *Trout Farm - Restaurant*

This *criadero* or trout farm is located a couple of kilometers outside Colonia Suiza. Situated on the shore of Lago Perito Moreno, they offer a tour of the trout farm. They sell delicious vacuum sealed trouts. They also have a restaurant open for lunchtime (closed Tuesdays).

Address: Beveraggi s/n, 8400 Colonia Suiza, San Carlos de Bariloche
Farm Hours: Daily from 11am to 6pm
Restaurant Hours: Daily from 12pm to 3:30pm, but closed on Tues
Call: +54 294-450-6411
Find them on Facebook: Facebook.com/Criadero-Truchas-Colonia-Suiza-172931659419199

Food Festival

Fiesta Nacional del Curanto

At the center of this festival is the ***curanto*** ceremony, where a giant meal is made at the "official" *curanto* at Restaurant Victor Goye. It is a rectangular pit of 3 x 8 meters (10 x 26 ft) where large hot stones are used to cook meat and vegetables covered by leaves. Many other curantos are made during the day to satisfy all the participants. Over the two days of the festival, you can enjoy the gastronomic fair and the local artisanal beers. The celebration also includes music and performances. The Fiesta del Curanto was declared a National Festival in 2013. It aims to celebrate the first settlers in the area and the importance of the indigenous culture in Argentine identity.

When: Two days in the first half of February
Where: Colonia Suiza
Call: +54-294-442-9850
FiestasNacionales.org/fiesta/177/Fiesta_Naional_del_Curanto

EL CALAFATE

El Calafate is an important tourist destination in Argentina: it is a central hub to visit the Los Glaciares National Park, including the world famous stunning glacier Perito Moreno and the Cerro Chaltén. It borders Argentino lake, which is the biggest freshwater lake in Argentina.

One thing to note is the high costs in this region. Patagonia in general, and El Calafate specifically, is expensive! It is the most expensive place in Argentina, costing even more than Ushuaia. That said, you can find great food and you need to be prepared to pay double the average price in Argentina.

FOOD STORES

The Big Stores

La Anonima

La Anonima is the major supermarket in El Calafate and in the southern part of Argentina. This particular store is very busy with tourists and not well stocked. It helps if you need last minute or basic items. However, for a better experience, skip this store and go to the next one below instead.

Address: Avenida del Libertador General San Martín 902, El Calafate
Hours: Daily from 9am to 10pm
LaAnonima.com.ar

Local Specialty Stores

Distrisur

Distrisur is a solid option in El Calafate for your grocery needs. It is a family and locally owned business. They carry fruits, vegetables, dairy, meat, wine, fresh artisanal pasta, and other produce. Definitively the best option in town.

Address: Casimiro Bigua 4, El Calafate
Hours: Mon-Sat, 8am to 12am; Sun from 8am to 2pm & 5pm to 12am
DistrisurelCalafate.com

Panaderías

Las Nonas Reposteras

Our bakery of choice in town: this is a small bakery that is always busy. You will find freshly made white and wheat bread as well as delicious pastry treats. Located in a back street near the city center.

Address: Julio Argentino Roca 1324, El Calafate
Hours: Daily from 7am to 1pm & 4pm to 8pm

María - Brownies y Algo Más

A small pastry shop at the entrance of El Calafate, they offer cakes, brownies, and other sweet delicacies. With a few seating tables, it is friendly place, located slightly outside of the tourist center.

Address: Avenida del Libertador General San Martín 524, El Calafate
Hours: Daily from 10am to 1pm & 3:30pm to 8:30pm; but closed on Tues.
Find them on Facebook: Facebook.com/Maria.BrowniesyAlgoMas/

Don Louis Panadería

This is the largest bakery in town with two locations. They also have a seating area where you can enjoy a drink with your pastry. They have a large selection of cakes, pastries, and bread. While large, the product and the service are not impressive.

Address: 9 de Julio 265, El Calafate
Second location at Avenida del Libertador General San Martín 1893, El Calafate.
Hours: Daily from 7am to 10pm
Find them on Facebook: Facebook.com/Panader%C3%ADa-Don-Luis-117088371639444/

Heladería

Ovejitas de Patagonia

This store makes artisanal *helado* (ice cream) and chocolates. Located in the center of the city, it is the best *heladería* in town and you will often have to wait in line. They also have a seating area to relax and enjoy your ice cream. Try the *Calafate Helado*, which has a deep reddish purple color. The taste is very fruity, deep and closer to a blackberry than a raspberry. Get ready to delight your tastebuds!

Address: Avenida del Libertador General San Martín 1197 El Calafate
Hours: Daily from 8am to 8pm
OvejitasDeLaPatagonia.com

Dulce de Lugar

This is the place to get the local speciality of Calafate: *alfajores*. You will also find chocolates as well. The production is done by hand in the back of the shop that can be seen from the inside. The store caters to tourists and has collections of packages with chocolate and *alfajores* for sale.

Address: Avenida del Libertador General. San Martín 1199, El Calafate
Hours: Daily from 10am to 1pm & 3:30pm to 8:30pm; but closed on Tues

RESTAURANTS

La Fonda del Parrillero

This is a friendly rotisserie in the city center where you will find *empanadas*, fresh pasta, cooked meats, *tortas* and sandwiches to go. There are a few tables to eat or lounge at while you wait for your order. Order the *bife de cordero* with fries and eat it with a fresh salad.

Address: 9 de Julio 29, El Calafate
Hours: Daily from 10am to 12am
Call: +54 290-249-3777
Find them on: TripAdvisor.com
Price Range: $

Kau Kaleshen

This friendly restaurant has a relaxed atmosphere, nice menu and wine selection, making it a popular recommendation from the locals. It is located two blocks from the city center. They also open in the afternoon for drinks and sweets. Their desserts are outstanding. Don't miss the apple pie.

Address: Gregores 1256, El Calafate
Hours: Daily from 4pm to 11pm; but closed on Tues.
Call: +54 290-249-1188
Find them on Facebook: Facebook.com/KauKaleshen
Price Range: $$

Mi Rancho

This is a very popular restaurant with locals and tourists alike. You want to make a reservation ahead of time. It serves local lamb specialities at a reasonable price in an intimate and rustic atmosphere. Order the lamb stew and be patient with the service.

Address: Gobernador Moyano 1089 Esq. 9 de Julio, El Calafate
Hours: Mon-Sat, 7pm to 11:30pm
Call: +54 290-249-0540
Find them on Facebook: Facebook.com/MiRanchoElCalafate
Price Range: $$

Pura Vida

A hip restaurant with a relaxed atmosphere, they have a friendly service with nice meals. They also offer a few vegetarian options.
Address: Avenida del Libertador 1876, El Calafate

Hours: Daily from 7:30pm to 11:30pm; but closed on Wed.
Call: +54 290-249-3356
Find them on Facebook: Facebook.com/PuraVida.RestoBar
Price Range: $$

USHUAIA

Nicknamed *El Fin Del Mundo*, Ushuaia is at the "End of the World." Capital of the Tierra del Fuego (Land of Fire), the city is a popular gateway to the Antarctic and the South Pole.

Nestled between snow-peaked mountains and the Beagle Channel that connects the Pacific and Atlantic Oceans, the food specialities from this region are influenced heavily by the natural resources available.

FOOD STORES

The Big Stores

La Anonima

With friendly and helpful staff and a store stocked with most of your needs, this might be the best La Anonima supermarket we had the chance to shop at in Argentina. The closest location to town is located at the beginning of the main street, San Martin. Go there to shop for dairy, produce, beer and wine.

The second location listed is close to the museum Maritime del Presidio.
Address: San Martin 1506, Ushuaia
Second location at Gobernador Paz 190, Ushuaia
Hours: Daily from 9am to 10pm
Gobernador Paz location has different Sunday hours, from 10am to 2pm
LaAnonima.com.ar

Carrefour

Ushuaia has a large Carrefour in town. Expect to find the usual industrial products that Carrefour carries.

Address: 12 de Octubre 169, 9410 Ushuaia
Hours: Daily from 9:30am to 10pm
Carrefour.com.ar

Local Specialty Stores

Panaderías

Panadería el Artesano

Located few blocks north of town, this bakery provides nice bread, *facturas* and

Panadería Eureka

With several locations in Ushuaia, this bakery is one of the largest in town. They have *facturas* and other pastries. They have a service for lunch and offer sandwiches as well as freshly baked bread.

sandwich options.
Address: Magallanes 1706, Ushuaia
Hours: Tues-Sun, 8am to 1pm & 4pm to 8pm

Address: Don Bosco y Campos 2901, Ushuaia
Hours: Daily from 7am to 12:30pm & 5pm to 8pm
PanaderiaEureka.com

Verduleria

Mendosur Verduleria y Frutas

This is a great local store where you will find the best vegetables and fruits in town as well as wines and some organic products

at a very reasonable price. Friendly staff.
Address: Magallanes 1706, Ushuaia
Hours: Tues-Sun, 8am to 1pm & 4pm to 8pm

Carnicería

Frigorifico Trelew

This is a large butcher that sells directly to the consumer at his *carnicería*.

Address: Kuanip 577, Ushuaia
Hours: Tues-Sun, 9am to 1pm & 3pm to 6pm
Find them on Facebook:
Facebook.com/FrigoTrelew

Dietética Sol de Abril

Located downtown, this small *dietética* sells health oriented products that you will not find at most other stores.

Address: 25 de Mayo 70, Ushuaia
Hours: Tues-Sun, 10am to 1pm & 4pm to 8pm

Rotisserie & Deli

Todo Rico a Las Brasas

This is a *parrilla* that sells grilled meat to go with fries or baked potatoes. They also have sandwiches and *empanadas*. This is a great alternative to restaurant (or when

you don't know what to cook). La Botica is their restaurant next door with a seating area; it might be worth a try!
Address: Magallanes 1695, Ushuaia
Hours: Tues-Sun, 6pm to 11pm

Lo de Quique

This local joint offers traditional Argentine specialities at very reasonable prices compared to the Ushuaia standard.

You will find *milanesa*, *tartas*, *empanadas*, pastas, and sandwiches as well as local beers and wines.
Address: Magallanes 2310, Ushuaia

Pescaderias

Ahumadero Ushuaia

This is an artisanal smoke house located on the upper side of town. They sell canned, vacuum sealed, and smoked seafood as well as lamb products.

Address: Shanamain 809 (corner of Av. Alem 999), Ushuaia
Hours: Mon-Fri, 8:30am to 6pm. Sat closed in the afternoon. Closed on Sun
AhumaderoUshuaia.com.ar

Pescaderia La Costa

This seafood store is located downtown Ushuaia. They have a fresh seafood section as well as a small deli section.

Address: Gobernador Félix Paz 345, Ushuaia
Hours: Mon-Sat, 9am to 7pm
Find them on Facebook:
Facebook.com/Pescaderia.LaCosta

RESTAURANTS

Ushuaia has a lot of dining options and you are sure to find a restaurant to your liking. It is an expensive city and this is reflected in the restaurant prices. You might want to avoid the main street downtown Ushuaia where restaurants cater mostly to tourists.

Maria Lola Restaurant

Perched on a hill with a great view of the Beagle Channel, this restaurant has nice seatings and a relaxed modern atmosphere. Go for the seafood, and try to avoid busy nights booked by tours or cruises.

Address: Gobernador Deloqui 1048, Ushuaia
Hours: Mon-Sat, 12:30pm to 2:30pm & 8pm to 11pm
Call: +54 0290-142-1185
MariaLolaResto.com.ar
Price Range: $$

Kaupé Restaurant

One of the best restaurants in town, located uphill, it is overlooking the Ushuaia Harbor. The dining room has a classic feel, with tables decorated with crisp white tablecloths. The chef, Ernesto Vivian, offers a solid fine cuisine with local seafood specialities such as *merluza negra*, *octopus*, and *centolla* **crab**. A great choice for a nice evening!

Address: Roca 470, Ushuaia
Kaupe.com.ar
Price Range: $$$

La cabaña Casa de Té

Give yourself time to relax here after hiking the Glacier Martial; this cozy tea house is located at the foot of the glacier. Order a *submarino* or a tea and try their *alfajores*.

Address: Luis F. Martial 3560, Ushuaia
Hours: Daily from 8am to 8pm
LaCabania.com.ar
Price Range: $$

4. RESOURCES
What You Should Know About Traveling in Argentina

CULINARY CULTURE IN ARGENTINA AND BEYOND
- Argentine Chefs and Legends
- Authentic Argentine Experiences in the U.S.

PRACTICAL TRAVEL RESOURCES
- Visiting Argentina - Visa
- Money Tips
- Transportation
- Communication/WiFi

HEALTH AND FITNESS WHILE TRAVELING
- Health Insurance
- Fitness on the Road

Culinary Culture in Argentina and Beyond

Argentine Chefs and Legends

Francis Mallmann

Discover the grilling techniques used in Argentina to make the meat so tasty and flavorful. From Francis Mallmann, learn more about Argentine *asado* grilling in his book **Seven Fires: Grilling the Argentine Way**. Francis Mallmann's restaurants stand out for their commitment to traditional Patagonian cooking methods.

Doña Petrona

Doña Petrona (June 28, 1896 – February 6, 1992) was the Argentine counterpart to Julia Child. Prominent in the 1950s, she developed simple recipes that encouraged homemakers to use modern appliances like the gas stove. Like Martha Stewart, she gathered recipes and clever housekeeping tips in her bestselling cookbook, **El Libro de Doña Petrona**, which continues in popularity half a century later.

Narda Lepes

Considered the modern version of Doña Petrona, Narda Lepes is a Buenos Aires-born chef and television presenter. Her best seller **Comer y Pasarla Bien** *(Eat and Have Fun)* brings together recipes from the basic to complex, cooking tips, and shopping and nutritional guidance. Her book won the prestigious Gourmet Cookbook Award, which is considered equivalent to the Oscars for cookbooks.

Get links to books mentioned at: authenticfoodquest.com/argentinabook

Gato Dumas

Gato Dumas (July 20, 1938 – May 14, 2004) was a celebrated Argentine chef and restaurateur. He opened a number of upscale restaurants in the 1960s and 1970s in Buenos Aires. While overseeing the restaurants, he published numerous cookbooks and produced television programs. In 1998, he established a cooking school in Buenos Aires. Gato Dumas' **Colegio de Gastronomia** is today one of the most prestigious culinary institutions in South America.

Authentic Argentine Food Experiences in the USA

Los Fuegos by Francis Mallmann, *Miami, Florida*

To experience open flame cooking, Francis Mallmann's first restaurant in the U.S. is now open in Miami, Florida. **Los Fuegos** opened in March 2016 and is located at Faena Hotel Miami Beach. If your travels take you to Miami, stop by Los Fuegos and experience an *asado* with an open-fire kitchen and local ingredients with a *gaucho's* touch.

> **Address:** 3201 Collins Ave, Miami Beach, FL 33140
> **Hours:** Daily 12pm to 5pm and 6pm to 11pm
> **Call:** +1 786-655-5600
> faena.com/miami-beach/restaurants-and-bars/los-fuegos-veranda
> **Price Range:** $$$

The League of Kitchens, *New York*

If you are craving an authentic Argentine experience, but are not planning a trip to Argentina, make your way to League of Kitchen. Based in New York City, League of Kitchens offers immersive culinary experiences, including Argentina with Mirta Rinaldi, their Argentine instructor.

Mirta will take you on a tour through Argentina by teaching you how to make many of the authentic and traditional dishes found in this book. Read articles about The League of Kitchens at **authenticfoodquest.com/argentinabook**.

Practical Travel Resources

Visiting Argentina - Visa

Good news: U.S. citizens can now visit Argentina without paying a reciprocity fee. As of March 2016, the Argentine government temporarily suspended the $160 reciprocity fee it had charged U.S. travelers since 2008. This is for U.S. passport holders who intend to visit the country for less than 90 days for tourist or business purposes. For more information check out the **consular section** of the Embassy of Argentina's website.

For citizens of other countries, please check with your respective embassies for visa questions and reciprocity fees.

Money Tips

Foreign Currency

Since taking over in December 2015, President Mauricio Macri has been making changes to the economy in Argentina. One of the big changes that will impact your travels is access to the dollar. Before the election of the new government, Argentina had struggled with high inflation and lack of access to U.S. dollars. This created a "blue market" where the U.S. dollar was highly sought after at prices almost twice the official exchange rate. For tourists, especially in Buenos Aires, this meant that you would constantly have people after you calling out *cambio, cambio, cambio* for U.S. dollars in exchange for Argentine pesos.

With the new President and administration, the official rate of the dollar has been brought up to closely match the blue dollar rate. Argentina is still struggling with inflation, though there seems to be optimism with the new administration. Be sure to do your research prior to your travels. No matter how you end up getting your Argentine pesos, be sure to use them all before you leave the country; it is unlikely you will be able to change them back at a decent rate.

Two-Tier Pricing

One thing that you will run into in Argentina is two-tier pricing. In certain regions of the country, like Patagonia and the Lake District, there is one price for Argentines and another price for "nonresidents" which is much higher. We run into this at some museums, national parks and monuments and with local airlines. Be prepared for this two-tier pricing.

Transportation

National Travel

To travel across the country, you can either use the airline system or the long haul bus transportation system. The airlines are subsidized by the government and local Argentines pay half the price of foreign travelers. For foreigners, in general it is more economical to travel by bus. Depending on where your travels may take you and the long distances, incorporate travel by air based on your travel schedule.

Airlines

There are two main airlines in Argentina:

- Aerolíneas Argentinas
  This airline is the most important carrier in Argentina and is backed by the government.
- LATAM Airlines
  LATAM is an Argentine private airline which has an alliance with American Airlines.

In general, all airlines in Argentina fly to and from Buenos Aires.

Long Haul Buses

This is a very popular way to travel in Argentina. The long-haul buses are convenient and comfortable. You will find many companies providing great service and competitive pricing. To see more about routes and prices, check the Omnilineas website: **Omnilineas.com**

You can order your tickets online or purchase them directly at the the bus stations. Keep in mind that sometimes companies offer limited discounted seats. Those are usually only available directly at the counter. Also, some companies will offer discounts if you pay cash. Be willing to negotiate. There are three main classes of service on the long-haul buses:

- ***Semi-Cama:*** this is the lowest class with a comfortable seat that does not recline much.
- ***Cama Ejecutivo:*** the seats are larger than *semi-cama* and recline almost to a full horizontal position.
- ***Cama Suite:*** This is the top of the line class and best for traveling long distances. The seats recline fully. Some buses have private TV screens, WiFi (not always working) and power plugs. Some companies will also provide entertainment onboard like playing bingo or other similar games.

In general, meals are not offered in *semi-cama* unless specified. For both *cama* classes, you will have meals served during your trip. All buses have a bathroom, though we would recommend to use them only if you really have to.

The buses stop throughout the trip and depending on the length of the trip you may be allowed you to get off for a simple break. At most bus stations, you will be charged to use the bathrooms. Be prepared with cash on hand as well as your own toilet paper.

> From a personal anecdote, the only time we were allowed to go for free was in Chile. We had left Argentina and just crossed the Chilean border. We woke up in the middle of the night at the bus stop to go to the bathroom. When we walked into the bathroom, we were surprised to see the price was ten times higher than usual. That's when we realized that the prices were marked in Chilean pesos, which helped explain the price differences. We didn't have any Chilean pesos on us and the lady didn't accept our Argentine pesos. As we were desperate to go, she was kind enough to let us go in. The lesson here is that if you are planning on crossing the border, have local currency with you.

Local Bus

In most of the large cities in Argentina, you will find good local public transportation. Local buses can get you to different parts of a city or a region safely and at a very reasonable prices.

Always inquire the local tourist office for the latest fare, bus routes and pricing system. Some cities offer magnetic cards for a very low fee that can be replenished as needed. This is helpful as it avoids the need of having to carry exact cash on hand.

Taxis, also called *remis*, are a great way to move around especially late at night when public transportation is limited. Always check the cost of your ride prior to getting in the taxi. Take only official taxis to ensure your safety.

Public Transportation in Buenos Aires

The public transportation system in Buenos Aires is very well developed. There is a nice metro system called *Subte* in the city, as well as a convenient bus system. There are also regional trains that will provide transportation to the suburbs of Buenos Aires.

While the metro is a flat fee for one ride, the bus system makes you pay regarding the distance you cover. You have to give the direction to the bus driver so he can charge you the appropriate fee.

There is a useful App called **Como Llego** in Buenos Aires that helps you create your itinerary and select which metro or bus to take. You can also use the web version at **ComoLlego.ba.gob.ar**

In general the public transportation is quite safe. Just be aware of pick-pockets and be really careful with your purse and bags on the trains and buses.

For more information and resources on how to use the public transporation in Buenos Aires check the tourist office website: **Turismo.BuenosAires.gob.ar**

Communication

Cell phone

You will find throughout this book phone numbers listed for the different places mentioned. The phone numbers are mentioned for international callers without your international exit code. It includes Argentina country code +54 with 9, then the area code; for example 11 for Buenos Aires. When calling in Argentina from a local SIM card, you will need to remove the 5 first digits and only use the last 8 digits. For example, while dialing in Buenos Aires, you remove +54-9-11 and only use the last 8 digits.

The best option for cell phone usage in Argentine is to get a local SIM card with either **Movistar** or **Claro**, the two main providers in Argentina. Get a pay-as-you-go plan and refill (*recarga*) airtime and data usage when they offer discounts (usually a few days after you activate your number or after a refill). For more information about cell phone usage in Argentina, see additional resources at **authenticfoodquest.com/argentinabook**.

WhatsApp

Many South American countries including Argentina use the application called **WhatsApp** (WhatsApp.com). This applications allows you to call and text message for free from anywhere when you are on a WiFi network. It comes very handy when you want to stay in touch with other Argentines.

WiFi

WiFi is available throughout most of Argentina, though you will find inconsistencies throughout the regions.

In Buenos Aires, most bars and cafés offer free WiFi. The connection can be quite inconsistent from one café to the other. You will see signs all over the town celebrating free WiFi from the government. While it is not glitch-free, it does work. For more consistent and reliable access, hotels, cafés and restaurants all have good connections.

Outside of Buenos Aires, most large cities offer good WiFi connections. When outside the main cities, the connection tends to get slower or can be unavailable for short periods of time. Our worst experience was in the Jujuy province where the WiFi was very slow or unavailable for long periods.

Health and Fitness While Traveling

Health Insurance

Medical care in Buenos Aires is generally good, including dental services. The level of care is equal if not superior to what you find in the U.S. for a much more reasonable price. However, quality and availability of treatment can vary outside the capital.

It is safe to contract with a travel and medical insurance that will cover you for your trip.

We personally use **World Nomads**. They provide great coverage for medical, travel and electronic equipment. We had to use their coverage for dental treatment in Buenos Aires and we were really satisfied with their service.

To get more information about travel insurance, see additional resources at: authenticfoodquest.com/argentinabook.

Fitness on the Road

Your foodie travels through Argentina will tempt you with an array of delicious and authentic foods on a regular basis. This does not mean that you have to let your health suffer or pack on unnecessary weight.

One of the great things about Argentina is that you will find many activities and possibilities for staying fit and healthy on the road.

The most basic way to stay fit on your travels is to simply put on your walking shoes and explore the city on your feet. If you want something a little more active, enroll in a tango classes, join a pick-up football game or take a fitness or yoga class.

One thing to note is that in Buenos Aires and in

Running Trail at Costanera Sur Ecological Reserve, Buenos Aires

many cities across the country, you will find public exercise machines usually located in a park. The machines are basic and are designed to work the upper or lower body using your individual weight for resistance. All machines come with a set of instructions and are free for anyone to use.

But since we primarily like to eat, we have 5 helpful eating tips to share from our article at authenticfoodquest.com/argentinabook, "**How to Stay Healthy as We Eat our Way around Argentina**":

1. **Exercise portion control by sharing meals.** In Argentina, the portion sizes are pretty generous. Often the dishes are large enough for 2-3 people. You can help manage your weight by either sharing your meals or only ordering one plate of the appetizer, main meal and dessert and sharing it. This way you get to taste more local specialities, while only eating a small portion. This tip alone will be good for your body and your wallet.

2. **Choose to walk instead.** The landscape in Argentina is diverse and beautiful. As you travel around through the country, the landscape varies and is breathtaking. Take advantage of moments like this to walk. Explore the local surroundings on your feet. Take in the natural beauty and be fully present. One advantage of walking is that it allows you to make room for even more delicious food.

3. **Enjoy the mineral waters.** One thing that is surprising about Argentina is that the locals do not drink water when they are out and about or at restaurants. The beverages of choice tend to be soft drinks, mate, beer or wine. As noted in Savor This, Argentina has many delicious waters. Keep hydrated with the mineral waters like Villavicencio or Eco de Los Andes. You can also choose the carbonated water or *soda* to enjoy as well.

4. **Make homemade meals.** One of the best parts about traveling through food is the opportunity to buy fresh produce from the local markets or stores. If you have the opportunity to cook on your travels, take advantage of these moments to not only eat healthy, but to deepen your connection with the food from the local area.

5. **Argentina is your playground; choose your sport.** Whatever sport you enjoy or however you typically like to keep fit and healthy, you can still continue it on your trip to Argentina. Traveling through food does not mean that you should abandon your fitness regimen. Find a studio, club or gym that has your activity and make that a part of your travel experience. What a great way to participate in your preferred fitness activity in a foreign language and place! Choose your activity and stay fit and healthy.

FROM OUR BLOG

Running in Buenos Aires and Around Argentina

Our favorite way of keeping healthy on the road is by running. It is an activity that we enjoy and one that does not need any equipment or club to join.

Before leaving the U.S. on the quest for authentic food in Argentina, Rosemary signed up to run the Buenos Aires Marathon in October 2015. This was done to keep us fit and healthy while eating our way through Argentina. While this goal kept us focused, it added the extra challenge of answering the question *"where should we go run"* every time we were in a new place or city.

With Claire acting as coach, running partner and run organizer, we were able to find running trails in Buenos Aires, Mendoza, Salta, Cafayate and Tilcara. Whether we were running for 45 minutes or 2½ hours, we always found trails or roads that were safe.

One unexpected aspect we had to adapt to was the change in altitude. Buenos Aires is relatively flat, with an altitude of about of 25 meters (82 ft) above sea level. As we made our way towards the northwest of Argentina, the altitude gradually increased. In Mendoza, the altitude increased to 747 meters (2,450 ft) above sea level, Salta was higher at 1,200 meters (3,937 ft) and Cafayate, even higher at 1683 meters above sea level. The most challenging place to run was in Tilcara at 2,465 meters (2,240 ft) above sea level. Here we needed time to adjust and acclimatize to the altitude change.

Through running we got to discover parts of the cities we would never have known had it not been for the need to train. Running also gave us the opportunity to enjoy the outdoors and beautiful landscapes.

If you are planning on running in Argentina, give your body time to adjust to the altitude, drink lots of water, wear a hat and use sunscreen liberally.

Rosemary did successfully complete the Buenos Aires Marathon, which was her 8th marathon and first in South America.

Acknowledgements

"And when you want something, all the universe conspires in helping you achieve it." —Paulo Coelho, The Alchemist

This quest would not have been made possible without the support of many. In all the big ways and seemingly small ways you helped, your support strengthened our journey.

The trip to Argentina would not have been possible without the support of our U.S. based friends who opened their address books and put us in touch with food-loving Argentinians. Thank you Maria Jose Goycoolea and Francisco Correa for the wonderful introductions in Argentina and beyond. Romina Bongiovanni, we thank you for introducing us to your mom Cristina Gonzalez. Her knowledge and passion exposed us to more than we could have imagined. Thanks to you Michelle Lavin, as a result of your connections, we experienced the best local and artisanal *dulce de leche* from TOTA. Special thanks to Zack Stratis for making the introduction to Stuart Sender. That led to a connection with Katja Emcke and an authentic *gaucho* experience at *La Manga* in the Pampas of Argentina.

In Argentina, we give our gratitude to the following people for sharing their favorite cuisines and local joints with us: Lucrecia Pisano, Sandra Gabarru and Fernando Rodríguez, Santiago Reig, Daggy Ford, Ale Evans, Eduardo Quesada, Oscar Vignart, Maria Ana Gianni, Julio Cornejo and Sharon Nieuwenhuis. A special thank you to Santiago and Maria Janariz for welcoming us into your family and sharing an asado with us. We are humbled and remain forever grateful.

To the chefs, cooks and experts we met on the road, thank you for sharing your passion for Argentine cuisine. A special thanks to Francis Mallmann for being so generous with your time, your local connections and insights on Argentine cuisine. Vanina Chimeno, thank you for opening your kitchen and for sharing your passion with us. Maria de Luynes, behind the scenes, you made things possible and for that, we sincerely thank you.

We are very grateful to our friends and family that have supported us along this journey. Our heartfelt thanks to Genevieve Rouger and Catherine Ndegwa for believing in us. To Rose and Lori Hannigan, thank you for letting us call your home, "our home." To Emily Kidd our editor, thank you for taking our words and making them sing.

Lastly, we give our gratitude to the Authentic Food Quest community. Your engagement, questions and desire to learn about authentic specialities fuels us, and it is as much your journey as it is ours.

About the Authors

"Go confidently in the direction of your dreams. Live the life you have imagined." —Henry David Thoreau

Rosemary Kimani and Claire Rouger started Authentic Food Quest in mid 2015. They want to inspire people to travel through authentic food. In doing so, their goal is for people to have deeper and more meaningful experiences through food on their travels.

They have an uncanny ability and curiosity to spot and discover the local and authentic foods of a region. They spent 6 months in South America traveling across the continent discovering and writing about the local specialties and authentic foods from the region.

Their quest for authentic food experiences continues to Southeast Asia, starting in October 2016. Following a similar approach, they will explore the traditional dishes and authentic foods of the region.

Prior to Authentic Food Quest, Rosemary and Claire held senior level positions in corporate America. As a former advertising strategy director, Rosemary worked on global brands in the U.S. and France to develop compelling connections between brands and consumers. Claire holds a M.S. in Mechanical Engineering and an MBA. She worked at Fortune 200 companies in the U.S. and France with her most recent experience in food equipment manufacturing.

Now digital nomads, Rosemary and Claire seek to inspire travelers to connect through authentic food experiences.

Rosemary and Claire at Cumana Restaurant, Buenos Aires

If you want to get tips to find authentic foods, subscribe to authentic food quest newsletter to stay up to date on the latest local food discoveries AuthenticFoodQuest.com/subscribe.

You can also connect with Rosemary and Claire at:
AuthenticFoodQuest.com

 Facebook: www.facebook.com/AuthenticFoodQuest

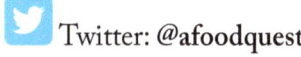 Twitter: @afoodquest

 Instagram: www.instagram.com/authenticfoodquest

 Pinterest: www.pinterest.com/afoodquest

 Youtube: www.youtube.com/c/authenticfoodquest

Savor The Adventure!

If you enjoyed the book, please take a few seconds to leave a review on Amazon.

www.ingramcontent.com/pod-product-compliance
Lightning Source LLC
Chambersburg PA
CBHW040329300426
44113CB00020B/2696